Crime and Criminals

OPPOSING VIEWPOINTS ®

OTHER BOOKS OF RELATED INTEREST

OPPOSING VIEWPOINTS SERIES

America's Prisons
Criminal Justice
The Death Penalty
Gangs
Gun Control
Hate Groups
Juvenile Crime
The Legal System
Media Violence
Teens at Risk
Violence

CURRENT CONTROVERSIES SERIES

Capital Punishment
Crime
Guns and Violence
Hate Crimes
Police Brutality
Prisons
Violence in the Media
Youth Violence

AT ISSUE SERIES

Does Capital Punishment Deter Crime?
Guns and Crime
Policing the Police

Crime and Criminals

OPPOSING VIEWPOINTS ®

Tamara L. Roleff, Book Editor

David L. Bender, Publisher
Bruno Leone, Executive Editor
Bonnie Szumski, Editorial Director
David M. Haugen, Managing Editor

OPPOSING
VIEWPOINTS®
SERIES

Greenhaven Press, Inc., San Diego, California

Cover photo: PhotoDisc

Library of Congress Cataloging-in-Publication Data

Crime and criminals / Tamara L. Roleff, book editor.
    p.   cm. — (Opposing viewpoints series)
  Includes bibliographical references and index.
  ISBN 0-7377-0121-8 (lib. bdg. : alk. paper). —
ISBN 0-7377-0120-X (pbk. : alk. paper)
   1. Crime—United States. 2. Criminal behavior—United States.
3. Juvenile delinquency—United States. 4. Crime prevention—
United States. I. Roleff, Tamara L., 1959–   . II. Series: Opposing
viewpoints series (Unnumbered)
HV6789.C6887 2000
364.973—dc21   99-29108
                                                           CIP

Greenhaven Press, Inc., P.O. Box 289009
San Diego, CA 92198-9009

"CONGRESS SHALL MAKE NO LAW. . . ABRIDGING THE FREEDOM OF SPEECH, OR OF THE PRESS."

First Amendment to the U.S. Constitution

The basic foundation of our democracy is the First Amendment guarantee of freedom of expression. The Opposing Viewpoints Series is dedicated to the concept of this basic freedom and the idea that it is more important to practice it than to enshrine it.

CONTENTS

Chapter 3: How Should Society Treat Juvenile Offenders?

Chapter 4: How Can Crime Be Prevented?

WHY CONSIDER
OPPOSING VIEWPOINTS?

"The only way in which a human being can make some approach to knowing the whole of a subject is by hearing what can be said about it by persons of every variety of opinion and studying all modes in which it can be looked at by every character of mind. No wise man ever acquired his wisdom in any mode but this."

John Stuart Mill

In our media-intensive culture it is not difficult to find differing opinions. Thousands of newspapers and magazines and dozens of radio and television talk shows resound with differing points of view. The difficulty lies in deciding which opinion to agree with and which "experts" seem the most credible. The more inundated we become with differing opinions and claims, the more essential it is to hone critical reading and thinking skills to evaluate these ideas. Opposing Viewpoints books address this problem directly by presenting stimulating debates that can be used to enhance and teach these skills. The varied opinions contained in each book examine many different aspects of a single issue. While examining these conveniently edited opposing views, readers can develop critical thinking skills such as the ability to compare and contrast authors' credibility, facts, argumentation styles, use of persuasive techniques, and other stylistic tools. In short, the Opposing Viewpoints Series is an ideal way to attain the higher-level thinking and reading skills so essential in a culture of diverse and contradictory opinions.

In addition to providing a tool for critical thinking, Opposing Viewpoints books challenge readers to question their own strongly held opinions and assumptions. Most people form their opinions on the basis of upbringing, peer pressure, and personal, cultural, or professional bias. By reading carefully balanced opposing views, readers must directly confront new ideas as well as the opinions of those with whom they disagree. This is not to simplistically argue that everyone who reads opposing views will—or should—change his or her opinion. Instead, the series enhances readers' understanding of their own views by encouraging confrontation with opposing ideas. Careful examination of others' views can lead to the readers' understanding of the logical inconsistencies in their own opinions, perspective on why they hold an opinion, and the consideration of the possibility that their opinion requires further evaluation.

EVALUATING OTHER OPINIONS

To ensure that this type of examination occurs, Opposing Viewpoints books present all types of opinions. Prominent spokespeople on different sides of each issue as well as well-known professionals from many disciplines challenge the reader. An additional goal of the series is to provide a forum for other, less known, or even unpopular viewpoints. The opinion of an ordinary person who has had to make the decision to cut off life support from a terminally ill relative, for example, may be just as valuable and provide just as much insight as a medical ethicist's professional opinion. The editors have two additional purposes in including these less known views. One, the editors encourage readers to respect others' opinions—even when not enhanced by professional credibility. It is only by reading or listening to and objectively evaluating others' ideas that one can determine whether they are worthy of consideration. Two, the inclusion of such viewpoints encourages the important critical thinking skill of objectively evaluating an author's credentials and bias. This evaluation will illuminate an author's reasons for taking a particular stance on an issue and will aid in readers' evaluation of the author's ideas.

As series editors of the Opposing Viewpoints Series, it is our hope that these books will give readers a deeper understanding of the issues debated and an appreciation of the complexity of even seemingly simple issues when good and honest people disagree. This awareness is particularly important in a democratic society such as ours in which people enter into public debate to determine the common good. Those with whom one disagrees should not be regarded as enemies but rather as people whose views deserve careful examination and may shed light on one's own.

Thomas Jefferson once said that "difference of opinion leads to inquiry, and inquiry to truth." Jefferson, a broadly educated man, argued that "if a nation expects to be ignorant and free . . . it expects what never was and never will be." As individuals and as a nation, it is imperative that we consider the opinions of others and examine them with skill and discernment. The Opposing Viewpoints Series is intended to help readers achieve this goal.

David L. Bender & Bruno Leone,
Series Editors

Greenhaven Press anthologies primarily consist of previously published material taken from a variety of sources, including periodicals, books, scholarly journals, newspapers, government documents, and position papers from private and public organizations. These original sources are often edited for length and to ensure their accessibility for a young adult audience. The anthology editors also change the original titles of these works in order to clearly present the main thesis of each viewpoint and to explicitly indicate the opinion presented in the viewpoint. These alterations are made in consideration of both the reading and comprehension levels of a young adult audience. Every effort is made to ensure that Greenhaven Press accurately reflects the original intent of the authors included in this anthology.

INTRODUCTION

"People naturally have this pessimism about [future crime trends].... If you predict the future's going to be terrible, you're in a win-win situation. If it does happen, you were right. If it doesn't, your raising the flag of concern helped turn it around."

—Howard Snyder, National Center for Juvenile Justice, January 3, 1999

In December 1998, the U.S. Department of Justice released statistics showing that the national crime rate had declined for the seventh year in a row. According to the FBI's Uniform Crime Report, the homicide rate fell 31 percent from its all-time high in 1991 and was at its lowest point since the 1970s. The violent crime rate also dropped dramatically—25 percent—falling to its lowest level since 1973, when the Justice Department began collecting crime victimization statistics. Property crimes dropped 17 percent from 1997 to 1998 alone, and by 55 percent since 1973.

However, some criminologists and social commentators contend that, despite the good news these figures seem to represent, there is still reason to be concerned about crime in the United States. These experts point out that while the overall crime rate is declining to levels not seen since the 1970s, the severity of crimes committed since then is much worse. Drive-by shootings, carjackings, and domestic terrorism were practically unheard of then, writes syndicated columnist Carl Rowan. "[Now] we live in a society where no family is immune to sudden death." Especially frightening to some are the juvenile offenders who show no fear of the law or mercy toward their victims. Princeton University professor John J. DiIulio Jr. calls these criminals "super-predators," claiming that they brutalize, maim, and even kill their victims just for the thrill of it.

The juvenile crime future looks bleak to some criminologists in other ways as well. Population experts predict the number of adolescents will grow by 16 percent between 1995 and 2010. Statistics show that most crimes are committed by male adolescents who learn their behavior from older criminals. Combining these two trends—an increasing number of violence-prone male adolescents who will learn about crime from older super-predators—DiIulio asserts that young boys in the 1990s are "a ticking time bomb." The falling crime rate in the 1990s is merely the "lull before the crime storm," he contends; when these young boys enter their adolescent years and begin their criminal careers, the crime rate will shoot back up again.

Some crime experts contend that the drop in crime rates may be due in part to inaccurate record keeping by the police. Lawrence W. Sherman, chairman of the University of Maryland's department of criminology and criminal justice, studied police reporting procedures across the country and discovered that no two police departments classified crimes exactly in the same way. For example, Sherman found that police departments may downgrade the classification of some violent crimes, such as aggravated assault, to a less violent crime, such as simple assault, which is not included in the FBI's violent crime rate. In 1990 in Illinois, rapes were categorized as "miscellaneous incidents." Sherman also claims that some police departments did not make written reports of all the crimes reported to them. On the other hand, he also discovered departments that overrated the seriousness of a crime. By not reporting some crimes and mislabeling others, Sherman contends that the police can "cook the books" to make themselves and their city look good.

Other criminologists claim that the nation's falling crime rate is nothing but good news for Americans. The crime rate has declined sharply for seven years, a fact they attribute to the declining use of crack cocaine which has reduced both the number of addicts stealing to support their habit and the number of dealers killing to protect their turf; harsher prison sentences that have kept criminals off the streets; and a booming economy that has provided a paying alternative to a life of crime. As for DiIulio's warnings of a growing "super-predator" population, some criminologists contend that those fears are unfounded. According to Franklin E. Zimring, a professor of law at the University of California at Berkeley, the link between an increasing juvenile population and a soaring crime rate has not been as strong in the 1990s as in past years. He points out that the juvenile crime rate has been falling since 1992 while the number of adolescents has been growing. He further notes that while a 16 percent increase in the number of adolescents between 1995 and 2010 is not insignificant, by comparison, the adolescent population that is probably responsible for much of the soaring crime rates in the 1980s expanded by 50 percent between 1960 and 1975.

Furthermore, crime experts contend that fears of a crime epidemic are fueled by the media, which exaggerate and emphasize crime in their news reports. Critics of the press claim that the media gave an inordinate amount of television time and newsprint to stories of children who killed their classmates and teachers between October 1997 and May 1998. During that time, fourteen students were killed in six separate incidents. Syndicated columnist James K. Glassman writes that these murders must be put into perspective:

> The United States has 38 million children between the ages of 10 and 17 and 20,000 secondary schools. In 1994, there were no school shootings in which more than one person was killed; [in 1997], there were four; [in 1998], two. In 1995, (the latest statistics), 319 kids aged 10 to 14 were murdered; the homicide rate for seniors aged 70 to 74 is 50 percent higher.

While the murder of these schoolchildren is a tragedy, Glassman concludes, it is not the epidemic the media make it out to be. Moreover, the media, by exploiting these stories, "may be helping to light the fuse" for other unstable teens who are "bombs waiting for detonation."

The media, juvenile crime, the growth and decline of the adolescent population, and police procedures are just a few of the factors that may have an effect on future crime trends. *Crime and Criminals: Opposing Viewpoints* examines differing opinions on the causes of crime and society's response in the following chapters: What Causes Crime? Does Controlling Guns Control Crime? How Should Society Treat Juvenile Offenders? How Can Crime Be Prevented? The authors in this anthology discuss differing views on the effects and social implications of crime in the United States.

|WHAT CAUSES CRIME?

CHAPTER PREFACE

Many Americans are appalled by the depictions of violence in the mass media and the entertainment industry. They believe that continual portrayals of murder, assaults, and other acts of violence in the media contribute to violence in real life. Critics point to several instances where actual crimes mimic the violence portrayed in movies, television shows, and other forms of entertainment. For example, two teenage brothers in Hollywood, Florida, who were charged in December 1998 with raping and sexually abusing their eight-year-old half sister, admitted to police detectives that they learned about incest and anal, oral, and vaginal sex by watching the controversial *Jerry Springer Show* on television.

Critics of the *Jerry Springer Show* and of similar forms of pop culture contend that portrayals of violence on television, in movies, in music, and in video games have a negative influence on society and especially on children. Exposure to violence has consequences, they argue, and some studies indicate that children who are continually exposed to violence become more aggressive and less sensitive to others' pain, learn that violence is an acceptable solution to problems, and are more likely to become criminals when they are adults. Leonard Eron, an authority on media and children, testified before Congress on his study: "There can no longer be any doubt that heavy exposure to televised violence is one of the causes of aggressive behavior, crime and violence in society."

However, some social researchers and media critics assert that Jerry Springer, movie and television directors, singers, and video game designers should not be held responsible for how viewers and listeners respond to the violence depicted in their talk shows, movies, music, and games. Each individual viewer is responsible for his or her actions, they argue, not the media. Some researchers question the validity of studies that show a link between media violence and crime. According to psychology professor Kevin Durkin, "The relationship between viewing and aggressive behavior is a weak one. No one has ever demonstrated otherwise." Furthermore, these analysts maintain that at least in the case of the two brothers, the children's parents bear much of the responsibility for not supervising their children more closely.

Experts are still debating whether violence in the media causes or contributes to crime in real life. The authors in the following chapter examine this issue and others as they explore the topic of what causes crime.

| "There is, in short, a scientific consensus that criminal and antisocial behavior have genetic, as well as environmental, sources."

GENETICS MAY INFLUENCE CRIMINAL BEHAVIOR

Richard J. Herrnstein

Richard J. Herrnstein argues in the following viewpoint that while environment may influence criminality, so, too, do genetic factors. Studies show that adopted children with a biological parent who is a criminal have an increased risk of engaging in criminal behavior. Furthermore, Herrnstein asserts, other studies have found that certain genetic physical traits, such as gender, muscularity, and an extra Y chromosome, also increase the risk of criminality. Therefore, he argues, it is irrefutable that criminal behavior has a genetic source. The late Herrnstein was the Edgar Pierce Professor of Psychology at Harvard University and a member of the American Academy of Arts and Sciences. He is also the coauthor of *Crime and Human Nature* and of *The Bell Curve: Intelligence and Class Structure in America.*

As you read, consider the following questions:

1. What are criminogenic traits, according to Herrnstein?
2. What effect does an extra Y chromosome have on intelligence, according to Herrnstein?
3. According to the author, what ratio of the general male population has an extra Y chromosome compared to the proportion of male prisoners with an extra Y chromosome?

Excerpted from Richard J. Herrnstein, "Criminogenic Traits," in *Crime*, edited by James Q. Wilson and Joan Petersilia (San Francisco: ICS Press, 1995). Copyright ©1995 Institute for Contemporary Studies. Reprinted by permission of the publisher. (Notes in the original have been omitted in this reprint.)

W ho commits crime? Our picture of the typical offender depends on how broad a brush we use to paint the answer. With too fine a brush, only the accidents of single lifetimes become salient—a harsh parent, an evil influence, a bad break or two that tipped the balance the wrong way. We may look at this picture and say that there is no typical offender, only atypical ones, each atypical in his or her own way. At the other extreme, with too broad a brush, only the general sociological forces emerge—poverty, inequality, oppression, racism, and the like. In this picture, an offender is typical only to the extent that he or she has been buffeted by those social forces. But between these two levels of description lies evidence showing offenders to be, on the average, something other than a random sampling of the population at large or of the populations subjected to the sociological forces. The focus of this viewpoint is on this intermediate level of description, where we seek the distinguishing individual traits of the average offender. These are . . . *criminogenic* traits.

To the extent that this intermediate level differs from the two on either side of it, the traits of the typical offender cannot be assumed to be caused either by how he or she was treated by society—by the educational system, by the job market, by the political system, by the law—or by accidental circumstances having led the offender astray. Social institutions, families, friends, even random events, matter, but they do not tell the whole story about the average criminal life. This viewpoint shows that the average offender is psychologically atypical in various respects, not necessarily to a pathological degree, but enough so that the normal prohibitions against crime are relatively ineffective. In designing public policy, we must bear in mind that a society that successfully keeps 80 to 90 percent of its population on the right side of the law may find that it needs other measures to deter the remaining 10 to 20 percent, for reasons that have more to do with individual criminogenic traits than with defects in policy. . . .

THE BIOLOGY OF CRIMINALITY

Some theorists criticize the search for the psychological characteristics of chronic offenders. Doing so, they imply, is like the wise men describing the elephant, each sedulously describing the trunk or the tail or the tusks or the ears, but all missing the beast. Instead, they suggest, we should be looking at the propensity for breaking the law, "criminality," as a trait in its own right. This is not unlike the approach in this viewpoint.

Yet, there are good pragmatic reasons for teasing out the specific psychological correlates. For one thing, there are established ways for measuring them. Insofar as "criminality" differs from the behavior of breaking the law, it is not obvious how to measure it. For another, we know something about the origins of intelligence, personality, and temperament. The evidence for a substantial heritability for IQ is no longer seriously in doubt. Personality has likewise been shown to have significant genetic involvement, although probably less so than IQ. Inasmuch as criminal behavior is associated with intelligence and personality, and inasmuch as personality and intelligence have genetic influences on them, then it follows logically, as night follows day, that criminal behavior has genetic ingredients.

DATA CONFIRM THE LINK

However ironclad the logic, it is reassuring to have it confirmed by data. The criminal behavior (or other forms of antisocial behavior) of parents is one of the primary risk factors for criminal behavior in their children. It may seem that this is more readily explained environmentally than genetically, but it is also true for children who are raised in adoptive homes by foster parents who are not offenders. Adopted children resemble their natural parents in their offending more than they resemble their foster parents. The more serious an offender a biological parent is, the greater the risks of crime in his or her adopted-away child. The more serious the offending of the adopted offspring, the more likely it is that there is an offender among the natural parents.

The data on adopted children resonate with the data on twins. If one twin is an offender, his or her co-twin is at risk for being one, too. If the twins are identical, then the correlation between them is significantly larger than if they are fraternal. Since identical twins share all their genes, while fraternal twins share about one half, a difference between fraternals and identicals in the correlation is evidence for a genetic ingredient in offending. The evidence has frequently been disputed on the grounds that it is the greater similarity of environments for identical twins that makes them resemble each other in antisociality, rather than all the genes they share. As a general argument against twin studies, this one has been largely refuted. The greater similarity among identical twins in personality and in intelligence is evidently caused primarily by their greater genetic overlap, not because they are treated similarly or share a family environment. One of the more unexpected discoveries of human behavior genetics of the past decade has been that the family environment develops psychological differences among the children growing up in it, rather than resemblances. Identical twins, in other words, resemble each other psychologically so much, not because of the family environment, but in spite of it.

On the other hand, data seem to indicate that this general finding may need to be qualified for criminal activities specifically. Lawbreaking activities are somewhat contagious, as anyone who has witnessed the looting and vandalizing mobs in urban riots should realize. On a microscopic scale, something similar may go on within families. Siblings (including twins) influence each other's tendency to break the law. If one sibling uses illegal drugs or commits other crimes, the chance that the other one will as well depends on how close a relationship and on how many mutual friends the siblings have. One plausible (though not the only) interpretation is that siblings reinforce or inhibit each other's behavioral dispositions toward criminal behavior, the more so the closer their relationship with each other.

Let us summarize by saying that the cognitive and personality dispositions toward antisocial behavior may be less influenced by

THE DANISH ADOPTION STUDIES

In a study of 3,691 adopted boys, those whose biological parents (usually fathers) had been convicted of crimes were more likely themselves to be convicted of crimes than were adopted children whose biological parents had had no trouble with the law. Neither the children nor their adoptive parents knew about the criminal records of the biological parents, so the children's actions did not result from parental expectations based on beliefs about inheritance.

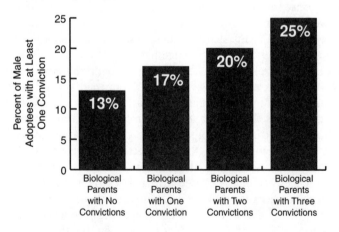

Dorothy C. Wertz, *Gene Letter*, November 1996.

the family environment than the acting out of the behavior itself. But this is not the same as saying that only the environment matters in determining behavior, as distinguished from dispositions. In adoption data, blood relatives act criminally in similar ways even though they have not shared a family environment.

Some commentators argue that behavior is too ephemeral to have genetic roots. This argument arises in a misunderstanding of how inheritance works, but perhaps such critics will be helped by the evidence of physical correlates of criminal behavior. No one doubts that physical traits may have genetic influences on them.

It has been shown repeatedly that offender populations are moderately atypical in physique. They are more likely to be mesomorphic (i.e., muscular, large-boned) and less likely to be ectomorphic (i.e., tall, linear bodies) than the population at large. Even among childhood delinquents, who are disproportionately nonectomorphic mesomorphs (i.e., chunky, large-boned, and muscular), the ones who go on to adult criminal behavior are still more disproportionately nonectomorphic mesomorphs. Why? One reason is that physique is correlated with personality and temperament, and that nonectomorphic mesomorphs are likely to have the traits associated with offending in higher frequency than the population at large. Another may be that children like this are generally more effective in acting out their frustrations and desires than delicately built children. Yet another may be the stereotypic expectations of people, based on their appearance. A strong-looking, large-boned youngster may simply look tougher to adults and his or her peers. He or she then learns to live up to the expectations, and vice versa for a delicate-looking youngster. Many chunky people, of course, do not become criminals, but the elevation of the risk among them is easy to substantiate, if not to interpret.

EVIDENCE OF OTHER CORRELATIONS

A growing scientific literature is replete with other evidence of correlations between offending or antisocial behavior and physical traits. I will run through a few of them, but note, first, that most of these correlations are *weaker* than the correlations with psychological traits. It has been shown that offenders have, on the average, lower heart rates than nonoffenders, and lower nervous system responsiveness to sudden stimuli. Their brain waves are more likely to have had atypical patterns in childhood. Neurological, biochemical, and metabolic abnormalities, some of which may be caused by abuse, injury, or disease, rather than genes, turn up disproportionately in offenders who are especially brutal or violent. An expected correlation has not been clearly substantiated: although a good many studies show some weak association between male hormones and criminal behavior or antisociality, many do not.

An association between criminal behavior and hormones was expected because few variables correlate as strongly with criminal behavior as sex, in our society and in every other one for which data are available. The changing woman's role in America has just barely narrowed the huge disproportion between male and female crime. The next section further discusses the sex difference in offending; it is noted here as yet another example of a physical variable that correlates with criminal behavior.

FEMALES, MALES, AND SUPERMALES

The disproportion in offending across the sexes varies with the crime, but it ranges from barely two to one for certain property offenses and vagrancy to well over fifty to one for overtly violent crimes. Men outnumber women in prisons by more than twenty to one and in jails by almost ten to one. As a rule, the more heinous the crime or more chronic the criminal, the greater the disproportion between males and females. The only major category of crime with an excess of female perpetrators is prostitution, which may say more about sexual behavior and about a criminal justice system that considers the seller of a commodity more culpable than the buyer than it does about criminal tendencies. While some have argued that the disproportionate antisocial behavior of males is a result of culture and learning pure and simple, by far the majority of experts grant that it has some genetic foundation. The sheer universality of the difference across time and place makes the purely cultural explanation implausible on its face. Yet, it has not been easy to pinpoint wherein the fundamental psychological differences reside, beyond noting that it is more likely to be in something that distinguishes the typical personalities of males and females than in their intelligence. The average female offender is more deviant psychologically than the average male offender, for a given level of criminal behavior.

THE EXTRA Y CHROMOSOME

Whatever differentiating genetic factor makes men more likely to be antisocial than women, it must ultimately arise in the chromosome pair that determines genetic sex. This pair is called XX in women and XY in men, referring to what the chromosomes look like microscopically. If one Y chromosome increases the tendency toward offending, it seems plausible that two should increase it more. Thus, it is not surprising that the discovery of XYY males in the 1960s prompted talk of "supermales" who were supposedly prone to frighteningly violent criminal behavior. The picture of an XYY male conjured up in the popular media looked like Boris Karloff playing Frankenstein's monster. This was certainly overdrawn, but now the pendulum has swung too far back. It has become commonplace to deny any correlation at all between the XYY syndrome and criminal behavior. In fact, there is a clear elevation of criminal behavior among the tiny population of XYY males. But the crime is, as far as has been shown in aggregate studies, usually (but not always) fairly ordinary, not excessively or preternaturally violent.

At the least the extra Y chromosome reduces IQ, and thereby elevates the risk of criminality. However, studies of other species have shown that the level of aggression displayed by males can be traced to genes on the Y chromosome. It therefore remains possible that an extra Y chromosome does something to personality and temperament to increase the tendency to break the law, as well as to IQ. The practical significance of the XYY syndrome is negligible, since it is so rare (probably fewer than 1 per 1,000 men). The theoretical significance is not small. Here is a genetic contributor to crime that is not hereditary, in the sense that it does not run in families; it pops up randomly across social classes and races, as far as is known. It increases the risk of criminal incarceration by a factor of about ten: the proportion of XYY male prisoners is about 1 per 100. The XYY syndrome is thus a natural experiment separating genetic from environmental factors, and the results of this experiment show decisively that criminal behavior can have genetic roots.

There is, in short, a scientific consensus that criminal and antisocial behavior have genetic, as well as environmental, sources. The disagreements among experts concern the size of the genetic factor. Some say it is negligible; others, that it may account for as much as 50 percent or more of the variance in criminal behavior. I will make no attempt to set a figure on the heritability of criminality or criminal behavior. For the purposes of this essay, it is enough to show that individual traits play a significant role in criminal behavior. For that proposition, it seems to me, there can be no doubt.

| "There cannot be a gene for crime because 'crime' does not exist as an entity and definitely does not exist as a biological entity."

CRIME GENE THEORIES ARE FLAWED

Jeff Milder

Theories advocating a connection between genetics and crime are misguided, argues Jeff Milder in the following viewpoint. "Crime" is a cultural concept, not a biological entity, he contends, and therefore there is no gene responsible for creating crime. Furthermore, Milder maintains, environment plays an important role in determining whether or not a person will become a criminal. Milder is a freelance writer.

As you read, consider the following questions:

1. What was the consensus of the Maryland conference on genetics and criminal behavior, in the author's opinion?
2. To what theory can genetic determinism trace its roots, according to Milder?
3. How would the discovery of a "crime gene" affect society's treatment of criminals, in Milder's opinion?

Reprinted from Jeff Milder, "Eugenics Resurrected: Is Crime in the Genes?" *Perspectives*, November 1995, by permission of the author.

In 1992, the Bush Administration began the Violence Initiative, a program intended to find genetic predispositions toward violence and criminal behavior and eventually to treat these with drugs and other therapy. Critics called the policy a revival of eugenics that would target poor minority children, and the ever-active nature-nurture debate about criminal behavior erupted again.

THE MARYLAND CONFERENCE

In September 1995, when scientists, philosophers, and psychologists gathered to discuss the state of research on the genetic basis for crime, people were worried. The Violence Initiative, after all, had been only the most recent example of a strident debate centering around such evocative catch-phrases as "eugenics," "the crime gene," and "genetic determinism." Minority groups, among others, feared that the conference, hosted by the University of Maryland and entitled "The Meaning and Significance of Research on Genetics and Criminal Behavior," would become a platform for issuing forth a new generation of doctrine and social policy based on the notion that criminal behavior is genetically or racially determined.

It did not. If anything, the conference put the brakes on the gung-ho optimism of earlier research linking socially deviant behavior to genes. By and large, biologists at the Maryland conference cautioned that little was known, and perhaps little could ever be known, about the biology of criminal behavior. Philosophers and social critics argued in favor of old-fashioned social remedies for crime—like education and counseling—rather than genetic solutions. The context in which these solutions were discussed is also significant: ideas were voiced by academics to fellow academics, and nary a word of this filtered out to the popular press.

While the fields of biology and psychology adjust their outlook according to new research, the American public still subscribes to an outdated paradigm in which criminals are born more than made and in which society treats them accordingly. This opinion continues to be the basis for harsh, discriminatory, and unproductive social policies.

THE FACE OF CRIME

Modern theories of genetic determinism (of which the genetics of criminality is only one) trace their roots to Darwin's *Origin of Species* and its notion that many characteristics of an organism are determined by its evolutionary past. The Italian anthropologist Cesare Lombroso proposed the first such theory about crime in the 1870s: criminals, he said, are relics of an earlier state of humankind and are therefore recognizable by certain "primitive" features. A sharp brow, a flattened nose (like a monkey), an "apish" appearance—these were dead giveaways of a criminal.

In the 20th century, genetic theories of crime assumed a façade of increasing scientific rigor. IQ testing and family tree reconstructions found that "social undesirability" often ran in families, and, though these results implicated environment as much as genetics in causing crime, they were used to justify prison sterilization programs in the 1920s. Chromosomes entered the picture in the 1970s when studies claimed that the XYY configuration (in which males have two instead of one Y chromosome) contributes to violent behavior: after all, males are more violent, so to be "doubly male" must make one more violent.

Recent theories have invoked specific genes, hormones and biochemical regulators to explain violent behavior. The pattern is an interesting one: as one buttress after another collapses, ever-more complex rationales for inborn criminality emerge. These modern theories are essentially new approaches to the old game of blaming individuals and not society for crime—the same game that Lombroso played. Obfuscated by biochemistry and modern technology, the new theories of genetic determinism are all but voodoo to non-specialists. Perhaps this is why they seem more believable, on the surface, than earlier, more accessible theories.

A KILLER GENE

The popular media does little to set the record straight. In the New York Times, on daytime talk shows, and elsewhere, headline-grabbing statements proclaim the iron hand of genes with alarmingly little discussion of the limits of behavioral determinism. New York Times science writer Natalie Angier's discussion of the genetics of mental illness is typical: "the evidence for a genetic contribution to [mental illness] is quite strong," she writes. "Studies of twins, for example, showed a hereditary contribution of anywhere from 30% to 50% for schizophrenia, somewhat more for manic-depressive illness." As most psychologists will point out, twin studies have so many caveats and are so few in number that they can hardly "show" anything; they may suggest a connection, but rarely anything so concrete as a number. It is not easy to write about the genetics of behavior for the popular press—and if one were to include in a story the appropriate cautionary notes, it would not make for a very attention-catching story. But this is no excuse for exaggerating scientific claims and misleading readers.

"Lower" forms of media are predictably more crass: Phil Donahue once alluded to the XYY chromosome as a way "to tell if your child is a serial killer." As sociologist Dorothy Nelkin laments, "the constant discussion of criminal genes creates the impression that it is only a matter of time before they can be isolated and used to predict behavior." These attitudes inevitably find their way into politics: in 1986, Mayor Ed Koch wrote that "certain individual biological—indeed genetic—traits, when combined with an uncertain moral environment, produce criminal behavior. Moreover, these traits can barely be changed, if at all." What are the important caveats that are being filtered out en route from the pages of Science and Criminology (which themselves often overstate the reliability of research) to the popular press and to public consciousness—and why should we be concerned with these detractors from nice, simple "truth"?

NOT SO BLACK AND WHITE

First, we have no suitable definition of crime that can be applied to genetic analysis. Many people might believe (correctly or not) that there is a genetic predisposition to murder or to rape. But what about shoplifting? What about Michael Milken's investment fraud? Few people would call this a genetically-based crime—and no researcher, to my knowledge, has bothered to investigate the heritability of white-collar crime. "Crime" is a cultural concept defined differently around the world; it is not a biological concept. There cannot be a gene for crime because "crime" does not exist as an entity and definitely does not exist as a biological entity.

Most genetic determinists are more subtle: they postulate the existence of genes for certain crime-encouraging tendencies such as impulsiveness and violence, not for murder, rape, or robbery itself. These theories are haunted by equally damning errors. Let's take the example of a commonly cited statistic: blacks in America are around 10% of the population but account for about one-half of all rape and murder arrests and about two-thirds of all robbery arrests. We could explain this fact in a number of ways: (1) blacks are more frequently the victims of economic inequality, and poor people commit more crimes than rich people, regardless of race, (2) blacks are treated by society in a way that encourages them to commit crimes, (3) blacks are more frequently arrested than whites for crimes they have committed or (4) that a large percentage of blacks contain genes predisposing them to crime. All of the ex-

planations (or a combination of them) could explain the correlation between race and crime. But which is correct?

Various studies have tried to decouple the effects of genes and the environment in causing criminal behavior. In 1984, a study of Danish males raised by adoptive parents (so that environment was partially controlled for) reported that children of repeat criminals were about twice as likely to be criminals themselves as the children of non-criminals. What about the effect of the environment? Crime statistics show that Texas's murder rate is four times that of Massachusetts, that rural areas have half the murder rate of large cities. Economic inequality is also highly correlated with crime rate. So, what if we were to compare the son of a rural Texas worker to the son of a Boston murderer—who would be more likely to commit a crime? It is apparent from this silly example that a statistic like the Danish study becomes relatively meaningless when placed in a world of confounding variables. To complicate matters further, we cannot be certain whether the sons of Danish criminals are more inclined toward crime because they possess a "crime gene" or for some other reason—perhaps the children are big and strong like their parents and therefore make more successful criminals. As in twin studies, the psychological effect of being raised by foster or adoptive parents is often overlooked. The point is that any supposed link between genes and crime carries with it many constraints—and these qualifiers are often ignored.

EMPOWERMENT, NOT IMPRISONMENT

The outcome of this scientific debate is not trivial; it is, and has been, the basis for social policies like eugenics and for our treatment of criminals. If we were to find a fairly rigid set of "criminal" genes, it might motivate us to lock up criminals for life or to execute them—after all, they will commit crimes regardless of how society tries to educate or reform them. It might also favor a system of "indeterminate sentencing" (such as the one the U.S. has) where a crime carries a range of punishments depending, among other things, on how likely the judge thinks the criminal is to commit future crimes. On the other hand, if it became apparent that criminal behavior is largely dependent on one's environment, we would spend more money on education, job training, and rehabilitation and expect a large dividend in the form of less crime.

This, notes Nelkin, has not been the prevailing attitude among most Americans. "The alarm over scientific theories that suggest a biological basis for violence arises in a political climate in which blame for crime, poverty and other social problems is increasingly placed on individuals, while responsibility for such problems is deflected away from society. By making social factors irrelevant, genetic explanations of crime provide convenient excuses for those seeking to dismantle the welfare state."

Disavowal of social responsibility underlies many of today's political decisions. New laws such as the "three strikes and you're out" crime policy and the "five years and you're out" welfare policy operate on the assumption that some people are just rotten apples, bound to end up in jail sooner or later. Admittedly, America has its share of incorrigible criminals and the lifelong unemployed. However, the lessons of behavioral genetics should tell us that, whatever a person's genetic predispositions, the effects of the environment are nevertheless very large.

The success of job-training and rehabilitation programs suggests that improving a person's environment is a boon even when that person belongs to a group or has genes that geneticists and psychologists call "crime-favoring." In light of the recent research in biology and psychology, this "paradigm of improvability" is clearly more appropriate than the old mentality of genetic inevitability. The task at hand—listen up, Phil Donahue—is spreading this wisdom from the academics at the Maryland conference to the people and the politicians of America.

VIEWPOINT 3

> "As the density of poverty increases
> in cities throughout the world, so
> will the density of joblessness, crime,
> family dissolution, drug abuse,
> alcoholism, disease, and violence."

POVERTY CONTRIBUTES TO CRIME

Douglas S. Massey

The concentration of poverty in cities during the twentieth century has also led to a concentration of crime and violence, asserts Douglas S. Massey in the following viewpoint. The poor frequently adopt a violent and aggressive demeanor in order to reduce their risk of victimization by criminals, an attitude which becomes ingrained and which can spill over into other areas of their lives. As the affluent segregate themselves from the impoverished, the problems of the poor will only get worse, Massey contends. Massey is the former president of the Population Association of America and a professor of population studies at the University of Pennsylvania.

As you read, consider the following questions:

1. Why was crime not as serious a problem among the poor in preindustrial times as it is in modern times, according to the author?
2. Why does the segregation of the affluent from the impoverished have a deleterious effect on the poor, in Massey's opinion?
3. What is Massey's vision of the future if class segregation is not reversed?

Excerpted from Douglas S. Massey, "The Age of Extremes: Concentrated Affluence and Poverty in the Twenty-first Century," Demography, November 1996. Reprinted with permission. (References cited in the original have been omitted in this reprint.)

P overty is old news. For thousands of years the great majority of human beings have lived and labored at a low material standard of living. In the first hunter-gatherer societies that emerged on the savannahs of Africa, in the agrarian villages that later appeared in the highlands of the fertile crescent, in the great agricultural empires that arose in Mesopotamia, the Mediterranean area, India, and China, most people were very poor. This iron fact of life prevailed in all human societies until quite recently.

Despite universal material deprivation, human societies evolved cultures and social structures that permitted people to live and reproduce in relative peace. Social order was possible in conditions of pervasive poverty because of one fundamental condition: The deprivation existed at low geographic densities. Under this circumstance, the socially disruptive correlates of poverty occurred infrequently and could be managed, more or less, through informal means; and because the poverty-stricken masses rarely came into contact with the tiny elite, they did not perceive the full extent of their relative deprivation.

POVERTY AND CITIES

The one place where rich and poor families came into direct contact was in cities, but preindustrial urban centers were few in number and never contained more than a tiny fraction of the human population. In premodern cities, moreover, the wealthy were constantly exposed to the poor and their privations, because preindustrial technologies permitted neither the separation of work from residence nor the segregation of the elite from the masses. Class integrity was maintained largely through social means, not physical separation. Indeed, the coexistence of poverty and wealth at high densities created problems of social order, as any student of ancient Rome can attest.

The industrial revolution of the nineteenth century upset the apple cart by creating and distributing wealth on a grand scale, enabling affluence and poverty to become geographically concentrated for the first time. Through urbanization, the rich and the poor both came to inhabit large urban areas. Within cities new transportation and communication technologies allowed the affluent to distance themselves spatially as well as socially from the poor, causing a rise in the levels of class segregation and a new concentration of affluence and poverty.

For a short time after World War II, mass social mobility temporarily halted the relentless geographic concentration of affluence and poverty in developed countries. The postwar economic boom that swept Europe, Japan, and the United States created a numerically dominant middle class that mixed residentially with both the upper and the lower classes. After 1970, however, the promise of mass social mobility evaporated and inequality turned with a vengeance, ushering in a new era in which the privileges of the rich and the disadvantages of the poor were compounded increasingly through geographic means.

A FUNDAMENTAL CHANGE

In the coming century, the fundamental condition that enabled social order to be maintained in the past—the occurrence of affluence and poverty at low geographic densities—will no longer hold. In the future, most of the world's impoverished people will live in urban areas, and within these places they will inhabit neighborhoods characterized by extreme poverty. A small stratum of rich families meanwhile will cluster in enclaves of affluence, creating an unprecedented spatial intensification of both privilege and poverty.

As a result of this fundamental change in the geographic structure of inequality, the means by which the undesirable correlates of poverty were managed in the past will break down. The juxtaposition of geographically concentrated wealth and poverty will cause an acute sense of relative deprivation among the poor and heightened fears among the rich, resulting in a rising social tension and a growing conflict between the haves and the have-nots. We have entered a new age of inequality in which class lines will grow more rigid as they are amplified and reinforced by a powerful process of geographic concentration. . . .

THE CONCENTRATION OF POVERTY

The advent of geographically concentrated affluence and poverty as the dominant spatial structure of the twenty-first century has profound implications for the nature of social life. Not only will the informal means by which past societies preserved public order break down and ultimately disappear under the onslaught of urbanization; they will be replaced by new cultural forms rooted in the ecological order of concentrated affluence and poverty.

Just as poverty is concentrated spatially, anything correlated with poverty is also concentrated. Therefore, as the density of poverty increases in cities throughout the world, so will the density of joblessness, crime, family dissolution, drug abuse, alcoholism, disease, and violence. Not only will the poor have to grapple with the manifold problems due to their own lack of income; increasingly they also will have to confront the social effects of living in an environment where most of their neighbors are also poor. At the same time, the concentration of affluence will create a social environment for the rich that is opposite in every respect from that of the poor. The affluent will experience the personal benefits of high income; in addition, they will profit increasingly from the fact that most of their neighbors possess these advantages as well.

DISADVANTAGED NEIGHBORHOODS AND URBAN CRIME

Predicted Property and Violent Crime Rates by Level of Disadvantage for White and Black Communities: Census Tracts in Columbus, OH, 1990

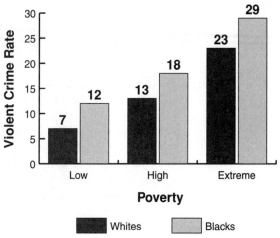

Lauren J. Krivo and Ruth Peterson, *Social Forces*, December 1996.

Therefore, in the emerging ecology of inequality, the social worlds of the poor and the rich will diverge to yield distinct, opposing subcultures. Among those at the low end of the income distribution, the spatial concentration of poverty will create a harsh and destructive environment perpetuating values, attitudes, and behaviors that are adaptive within a geographic niche of intense poverty but harmful to society at large and destructive of the poor themselves. At the other end of the hierarchy, a contrasting subculture of privilege will emerge from the spatial niche of concentrated affluence to confer additional advantages on the rich, thereby consolidating their social and economic dominance.

Perhaps no consequence of concentrated poverty is as destructive as the proliferation of crime and violence. Criminal behavior is associated strongly with income deprivation; thus the geographic concentration of poverty will cause a concentration of criminal violence in poor neighborhoods. According to estimates I developed for Philadelphia, every one-point increase in the neighborhood poverty rate raises the major crime rate by 0.8 point. Lauren J. Krivo and Ruth D. Peterson use data from Columbus, Ohio, to show that moving from a neighborhood where the poverty rate is under 20% to a neighborhood where it is over 40% increases the rate of violent crime more than threefold, from around 7 per thousand to about 23 per thousand.

How will the poor adapt to an environment where violence is endemic and the risk of victimization great? At the individual level, a logical adaptation is to become violent oneself. As my colleague Elijah Anderson has discovered through his ethnographic fieldwork, one can deter potential criminals and increase the odds of survival by adopting a threatening demeanor, cultivating a reputation for the use of force, and backing that reputation with selective violence. In a social world characterized by endemic violence, an obsessive concern with respect becomes a viable adaptive strategy.

Therefore, given the progressive concentration of violence, some poor people certainly will adopt violent attitudes and behavior as survival strategies. As more people adopt more violent strategies for self-preservation, the average level of violence in poor neighborhoods will rise, leading others to adopt still more violent behavior. As the average level of violence rises over time, more people will adopt increasingly violent strategies to protect themselves from the growing threat of victimization, and ultimately will produce a self-perpetuating upward spiral of violence.

The fundamental need to adapt to structurally embedded conditions of endemic violence leads to the emergence of a "code of the streets" that encourages and promotes the use of force. Asking residents of poor neighborhoods to choose a less violent path or to "just say no" to the temptation of violence is absurd in view of the threatening character of the ecological niche they inhabit. To survive in such areas, one must learn and (to a significant extent) internalize the code of violence described by Anderson. In this way, aggression is passed from person to person in a self-feeding, escalating fashion.

THE EFFECT ON THE BRAIN

Recent brain research suggests that this internalization of violence is more than a socially learned reaction that one can set aside whenever the situation warrants. Repeated exposure to

high levels of danger and physical violence wire emotional predispositions to rage and violence directly into the brain and
make them an organic part of a person's makeup. Research has
shown that perceptions of danger are channeled directly to a
small mass of neural cells known as the amygdala, which sits
above the brain stem near the bottom of the limbic ring. The
amygdala is capable of generating an emotional response that
triggers aggressive, violent behavior without passing through
the neocortex, the center of rational thought.

Emotional responses developed through the limbic system
are learned, but they are unconscious and automatic. Perceptions of danger may be signaled not only by physical threats but
also by symbolic injuries to self-esteem or dignity. The threat
triggers the amygdala to produce a limbic surge, which releases
catecholamines to generate a quick rush of energy lasting minutes. At the same time, the amygdala activates the adrenocortical
system to produce a general state of readiness that lasts for
hours or even days. Adrenocortical arousal, in turn, lowers the
subsequent threshold for anger and increases the intensity of
emotions, raising the odds that the rational centers of the brain
will be overwhelmed by powerful emotions beyond the control
of the neocortex.

By dramatically increasing the exposure of the poor to violence from a very early age, the new ecological order will maxi-
mize the number of people with hair-trigger tempers and ele-
vated predispositions to violence. These emotional reactions,
moreover, will not be turned on and off easily and rationally in
response to shifting social contexts. People who grow up in areas
of concentrated poverty and violence will experience profound
spillover effects in other areas of life: Disagreements with bosses,
spouses, and children will be more likely to turn violent, and
thus the odds of successful employment, marriage, and childrear-
ing will be diminished. Concentrated poverty is a stronger predictor of violent crime than of property crime, and of violence
between people known to one another than between strangers.

EDUCATION

The contrasting ecologies of affluence and poverty will also
breed opposing peer subcultures among rich and poor youths.
As affluence grows more concentrated, the children of the privi-
leged will socialize increasingly with other children of well-
educated and successful parents. Knowledge of what one does to
prepare for college and an appreciation of the connection between schooling and socioeconomic success will be widespread

in the schools of the affluent. Students will arrive in the classroom well prepared and ready to learn. School officials need only build on this base of knowledge and motivation by using their ample resources to hire well-informed guidance counselors and enthusiastic, talented teachers.

POVERTY TIED TO HIGH CRIME IN URBAN COMMUNITIES

Violent crime rates have more to do with poverty levels in a neighborhood than with the race of local residents, new research has found. . . .

"There are still many people who mistakenly believe there is something about Black neighborhoods that make them more violent and prone to crime," said Lauren Krivo, co-author of the study [on crime and poverty] and associate professor of sociology at Ohio State University. "Our research shows that neighborhoods with the most crime tend to be those with the highest rates of poverty and other types of disadvantage—regardless of whether they are predominantly Black or white."

New York Amsterdam News, March 15, 1997.

Meanwhile, the children of the poor increasingly will attend schools with children from other poor families, who themselves are beset by multiple difficulties stemming from a lack of income. Parents will be poorly educated and will lack adequate knowledge about how to prepare for college. Children will not fully appreciate the connection between education and later success. Supervision and monitoring of students will be difficult because so many come from single-parent families, and the schools will be unable to offset this deficit because of funding limitations. Students will arrive in the classroom poorly prepared, and neither the dispirited guidance counselors nor the overworked, underpaid teachers will expect much from the students.

In such settings an alternative status system is almost certain to develop. Under circumstances where it is difficult to succeed according to conventional standards, the usual criteria for success typically are inverted to create an oppositional identity. Children formulate oppositional identities to preserve self-esteem when expectations are low and when failure by conventional standards is likely. Thus, in areas of concentrated poverty, students from poor families will legitimize their educational failures by attaching positive value and meaning to outcomes that affluent children label deviant and unworthy. In adapting to the environment created by concentrated poverty, success in school will be devalued, hard work will be regarded as selling out, and any display of learning will be viewed as uncool.

Oppositional subcultures already have become entrenched in many black inner-city areas of the United States, where high levels of racial segregation have produced unusually high concentrations of poverty and educational distress. Once such a subculture becomes established, it acquires a life of its own that contributes independently to the perpetuation of educational failure, the reproduction of poverty, and the cultural transmission of low socioeconomic status from person to person, family to family, and group to group.

INTO THE AGE OF EXTREMES

Thus a new age of extremes is upon us. In the social ecology now being created around the globe, affluent people increasingly will live and interact with other affluent people, while the poor increasingly will live and interact with other poor people. The social worlds of the rich and the poor will diverge, creating the potential for radical differences in thought, action, values, tastes, and feelings, and for the construction of a new political geography that divorces the interests of the rich from the welfare of the poor. For the first time in human history, the advantages and disadvantages of one's class position in society will be compounded and reinforced by a systematic process of geographic concentration. . . .

The effects of ongoing urbanization, rising income inequality, and growing class segregation are exacerbated by racial segregation so that the effects are most salient and most visible among African Americans, but the basic processes are sweeping the world and concentrating poverty everywhere. In presenting the arguments at a general level, I seek to create a theoretical link between violence in Harlem and disorder in the slums of Rio and Mexico City, between social breakdown on the South Side of Chicago and the collapse of authority in rapidly urbanizing societies of Africa. In my view, the spatial concentration of poverty is implicated in the escalation of crime, disease, family breakdown, and the proliferation of various social pathologies throughout the world.

I also believe that social scientists' attention has concentrated too narrowly on the poor and their neighborhoods. Our obsessive interest in the generation and reproduction of class is rarely focused on the affluent. Scores of ethnographers descend on the homes, bars, and street corners of the poor to chronicle their attitudes and behavior; few attempt to infiltrate the mansions, clubs, and boutiques of the wealthy to document the means by which they maintain and reproduce their affluence. The concentration of affluence and poverty means that the social lives of the rich and the poor increasingly will transpire in different venues; we must study both in order to fully comprehend the newly emerged system of stratification. . . .

I believe that the concentration of poverty is a primary force behind the spread of new diseases such as AIDS and the resurgence of old ones such as tuberculosis; it also stands behind the creation and perpetuation of joblessness and the decline of marriage among the poor. It is implicated as well in the increase in unwed childbearing, and I believe it contributes to the spread of homelessness around the United States and the world. No doubt concentrated poverty also can be implicated in a variety of other social and economic phenomena in ways that have yet to be discovered.

Although I have attempted to explain how our social world has been transformed by the forces of spatial redistribution, it is more difficult to describe how the harmful social consequences of this transformation might be avoided. Confronting the new ecology of inequality is particularly difficult because concentrated poverty creates an unstable and unattractive social environment that is at once a cause and a consequence of class segregation. The social chaos stemming from concentrated poverty propels the affluent further into geographic and social withdrawal, and their departure further isolates the poor and stokes the fires of social disorder. Insofar as racial and ethnic segregation perpetuate concentrated poverty and its consequences in minority communities, the proliferation of antisocial behaviors will fuel pejorative stereotypes and intensify prejudice, making political solutions so much more difficult.

A BLEAK FUTURE

How does the future look to me? Bleak, because I know that it is in the elite's narrow self-interest to perpetuate the status quo. Addressing serious issues such as increasing income inequality, growing class segregation, racial prejudice, and the geographic concentration of poverty will inevitably require sacrifice, and the immediate course of least resistance for affluent people will always be to raise the walls of social, economic, and geographic segregation higher in order to protect themselves from the rising tide of social pathology and violence.

If the status quo indeed is the most likely outcome, inequality will continue to increase and racial divisions will grow, creating a volatile and unstable political economy. As class tensions rise, urban areas will experience escalating crime and violence punctuated by sporadic riots and increased terrorism as class tensions rise. The poor will become disenfranchised and alienated from mainstream political and economic institutions, while the middle classes will grow more angry, more frustrated, and more politically mobilized. The affluent will continue to withdraw socially and spatially from the rest of society, and will seek to placate the middle classes' anger with quick fixes and demagogic excesses that do not change the underlying structure responsible for their problems.

This scenario is by no means inevitable, and I sincerely hope it will not come to pass. Yet we are headed in this direction unless self-conscious actions are taken to change course. A principal motivation for my pessimistic candor and perhaps overly brutal frankness is to galvanize colleagues, students, politicians, and reporters into action. Until now, neither the nature of the new ecological order nor its social implications have been fully realized; my purpose here is not to offer facile solutions to difficult problems, but to begin a process of serious thought, reflection, and debate on the new ecology of inequality, from which solutions ultimately may emerge. Until we begin to face up to the reality of rising inequality and its geographic expression, no solution will be possible.

"Poverty does not cause crime—if it did, then it would be women, not men, making up 98% of the prison population."

POVERTY DOES NOT CAUSE CRIME

The John Howard Society of Alberta

In the following viewpoint, the John Howard Society of Alberta argues that although many convicted criminals grew up in an impoverished home, poverty itself does not cause crime. Many conditions inherent in poverty—such as inadequate housing and little adult supervision of children—may be risk factors for criminal behavior, but do not guarantee it, the society asserts. The fact that most convicted criminals are from poor families may say more about the criminal justice system than it does about the cause of crime, the authors contend. The John Howard Society of Alberta is a Canadian organization that provides legal and support services for current and ex-convicts and their families.

As you read, consider the following questions:

1. If poverty caused crime, what crimes would be nonexistent, according to the author?
2. What two elements must be present for a youth to be considered "at risk," according to Rolf Loeber?
3. What are the three basic definitions of poverty, according to the society?

Excerpted from "Crime Prevention Through Social Development: A Literature Review," by The John Howard Society of Alberta, at http://www.acjnet.org/cgi-bin/legal/legal.pl?lkey=no&ckey=jhslitre&tkey=docs. Reprinted with permission. (In-text references cited in the original have been omitted in this reprint.)

"Causes" is not the most accurate word to use when talking about factors commonly associated with delinquent behaviour. A cause-and-effect mind-set makes it too easy to assume that the existence of a risk factor inevitably leads to criminality. Besides raising significant ethical concerns, any Crime Prevention Through Social Development (CPSD) program designed on the basis of such a simplistic assumption would be doomed to fail from the start.

A COMPLEX PROBLEM

The evolution of a connection between actual criminal behaviour and an individual's life experiences and social and economic circumstances is far too complex and unpredictable to be attributed simply to cause-and-effect. Poverty does not cause crime—if it did, then it would be women, not men, making up 98% of the prison population in Canada. If poverty caused crime, white collar crime such as embezzlement or computer fraud and environmental crimes by industry would be nonexistent. Nonetheless, poverty during childhood is a recurring theme in the stories of so many persistent offenders that it is considered a significant risk factor, especially when in conjunction with other stress factors in a person's life, such as violence, unemployment or substance abuse. While social factors can combine to increase the likelihood of a person becoming delinquent, experience has also shown that being poor, a single mother and living in a disadvantaged area, for instance, still does not inevitably produce delinquent behaviour.

Research into risk factors and anti-social behaviour in children also emphasizes the importance of making a distinction between influence and cause. While behaviour problems in early childhood may influence future antisocial behaviour, such early behaviour problems do not necessarily cause later criminality. The route from disadvantaged child to delinquent youth is not a straight line. The complex problems of at-risk youth, for instance, have been described by William H. Kolberg as "a circle of antisocial and self-destructive behaviour. Young persons may enter the circle at any point, by using drugs, for example, or by committing petty crimes or dropping out of school. If they persist in such activity, however—if they remain on the circle— some or all of the other types of antisocial behaviour will begin to appear in their lives."

Such descriptions not only emphasize the non-linear process of becoming delinquent, but the need for an equally non-linear and long term approach to crime prevention. How clearly this non-linear relationship between risk factors and potential criminality is understood and applied at the policy development and program planning stages will determine how effective the implementation of CPSD initiatives will be in the long run.

DEFINING "AT RISK"

The term "at risk," whether pertaining to individuals, groups or communities, is a key definition in research into the effects of underlying social factors and criminal behaviour. Having a clear understanding of what at risk means and why it happens is essential to the CPSD process of implementing targeted programs which effectively address the underlying factors contributing to crime. One municipal task force on safer cities defines "at risk" as:

> Individuals or groups who are at greater risk of becoming involved in crime because of early life experiences, family characteristics, social factors in their community, or lack of positive opportunities.

"At risk" is frequently used in reference to a specific group, as in at-risk parents, at-risk youth and at-risk population. For example, Kolberg uses the term "at-risk youth" to describe young people who are at risk of being early school leavers and unemployed and who he sees as being "very much at risk of leading lives marred by crime and violence." Rolf Loeber examines risk factors in the development of anti-social behaviour in children and defines risk as having two elements: exposure and influence. A child must be exposed to the risk factor, and such exposure must influence the child's likelihood of engaging in anti-social behaviour.

There is no one factor which is more likely than any other to contribute to crime. . . .

POVERTY

Poverty is often cited as a factor associated with crime, although the link between poverty and crime has not been consistently established by research. The three basic definitions of poverty in current use are absolute poverty, relative poverty and exclusionary poverty. Absolute poverty refers to those without the most basic resources for survival such as food, shelter and clothing. Starvation is the basic measure in this definition. For families living in absolute poverty, the sole daily preoccupation is the struggle to find enough food and water to survive another day. The tendency has been to maintain that absolute poverty is exceedingly rare in a country like Canada. Yet, the number of people living on the streets is growing and while it is known that people are dying from starvation and inadequate shelter, especially during Canadian winters, the number of these casualties remains unknown.

Relative poverty refers to families and individuals whose income and other resource levels are scant in comparison to the majority of people in Canadian society. The number of people living in relative poverty fluctuates with economic conditions. The measure of relative poverty is the number of people living below a certain percentage of the average income level of the rest of the country. This arbitrary measure can mask the real circumstances in which many "poor" people are living, because income is not an accurate indicator of quality of life. While low income may not result in starvation, it can negatively affect development and future opportunities, barring impoverished persons from full participation in society.

EXCLUSIONARY POVERTY

Exclusionary poverty refers to persons excluded from our society's basic living requirements and opportunities. Exclusionary poverty more accurately depicts the quality of life of people living in poverty because it transcends simple economic considerations. Rather, exclusionary poverty looks at an individual's access to transportation, opportunities for socializing and participating in community life, health care and quality of diet.

TOO MUCH, NOT TOO LITTLE

In June 1997, *People* magazine put "Kids without a conscience" on its cover, citing horrendous teen-agers, mostly from affluent suburbs, who committed the most despicable crimes. Americans, who have been told for so long that crime is caused by poverty, may have to rediscover an ancient truth: that the greatest evil comes from those who have too much, not too little.

Jim Pinkerton, *USA Today*, July 14, 1997.

Statistics Canada defines a family spending on average more than 57% of its income on food, clothing and shelter as "poor." This Low-Income Cut-Off measure is the most widely accepted relative poverty measure and it varies by family size, by region and by rural or urban location. Low-Income Cut-Off figures are also called "poverty lines" in many reports, even though Statistics Canada no longer calculates poverty lines.

Another often-used method of measuring the poverty level calculates the incidence of poverty in a specific year. However, this gives an incomplete picture of poverty in Canada because it looks only at a few characteristics of poverty over a short time. The Economic Council of Canada carried out a study to find out about the poverty that families experience over time, which is a perspective usually concealed by traditional methods of measuring poverty.

LINKS TO CRIME

Despite the fact that research has failed to demonstrate an impoverished individual's greater likelihood of criminal involvement and that white collar crime proves contradictory, poverty continues to be linked to crime. Even studies using unemployment or the poverty line as measures show inconsistent results. Further, while researchers take increasing care to warn against simplistic correlations which equate poverty with crime, there is considerable consensus that living in poverty greatly increases the risk of criminality. The relationship between poverty and criminal behaviour is complex and unpredictable. There are too many variables involved and such a variety of different ways individuals cope with poverty that it is not possible to talk of poverty strictly in terms of being a risk factor.

However, history has shown that many of the conditions arising from living in poverty can increase the risk of becoming involved in crime, especially for children. For example, inadequate housing is often associated with poverty and crime. Inadequate housing, according to Larrie Taylor Architect Ltd., may be defined as "accommodation that does not meet basic physical standards of safety, sanitation, maintenance, privacy, access, adequacy and/or affordability." The Mayor's Task Force on Safer Cities' Housing and Urban Development Committee asserts that inadequate housing contributes to social problems including substance abuse, family violence and prostitution. Further, one study found that residents of public housing developments in the United States are more vulnerable to criminal victimization than other Americans. Five physical characteristics of public housing developments which may contribute to crime have been identified in the literature:

(1) restricted surveillance of certain areas within the projects; (2) insufficient "target hardening" measures to prevent burglaries; (3) lack of controlled access to project grounds and buildings; (4) the absence of controlled pedestrian circulation routes; and (5) insecure public transportation waiting facilities.

Other conditions associated with poverty include poor nutrition and health, chronic stress, problems with school, child abuse and neglect, family violence, inconsistent or poor parenting skills, psychological disorders and early childhood behavioural disorders. Research has demonstrated a relationship between these risk factors and crime.

THE CRIMINAL JUSTICE SYSTEM

That those living in poverty continue to be over-represented in Canada's crime statistics tends to say more about the criminal justice system and how it keeps official statistics than it does about any link between poverty and crime. Juvenile delinquency, for instance, is not exclusive to poor or working class youth. Self-report studies of adolescents indicate that at least 90% of high school boys engage in some delinquent behaviour. What makes it easier for people to believe that impoverished youth are responsible for the youth crime problem is the fact that the majority of incarcerated young persons are from poor families. However, this only represents those caught and incarcerated, not the overall youth population that commits crime.

THE WELL-TO-DO AND CRIME

Poor people are not more likely to engage in crime than are middle-class and upper-class people. The well-to-do steal far more from the American people with tax evasion, fraud, embezzlement and other forms of white-collar crime than do the poor with their strong-arm robberies, purse snatchings and burglaries. One survey by a George Washington University professor concluded that two-thirds of the Fortune 500 companies had committed one or more "significant illegalities" over a 10-year period. Accusing the poor of being more prone to crime than are others not only unfairly denigrates the poor. It also lets the non-poor off the hook—especially the wealthy who commit the most costly crimes.

Wade Hudson, Economic Security for All: How to End Poverty in the United States, 1996.

Why youths from low-income families make up a larger proportion of the statistics on juvenile offenders is still the subject of much debate. Reasons given range from the criminal justice system's inherent inequity and discrimination against the disadvantaged to an inevitable, cumulative effect of various stresses that result from living in poverty. Also, middle- and upper-income youth simply have access to more money and parental supervision. A youth from a low-income family may have less parental supervision because of the time constraints experienced by a working single parent. This youth is also less likely to have the money to participate in school sports or community recreation activities, so would be more susceptible to dropping out of school. Poor families also experience greater difficulty raising children, as low income often deprives the family of many opportunities and necessities associated with basic child rearing.

FAMILY STRESS

Continued economic hardship, combined with health problems resulting from malnourishment and chronic stress, puts strains on family relationships that may lead to family breakdown. This, in turn, can further add to stress from the difficulties of a sole parent trying to raise children. Unsatisfactory living conditions are particularly stressful during pregnancy. Fetal development is negatively affected by maternal stress. Such stress has shown to be closely related to ill-health, neurological problems, slow development and behaviour disturbances in children.

The CPSD programs with the greatest chance of making a difference in the long run will be those which target those most vulnerable to living in poverty and the multitude of problems arising from it. This will mean designing initiatives specifically for those experiencing such problems as poor nutrition and health, child abuse and neglect, woman abuse and family violence, poor parenting skills, inadequate and unsafe housing and poor school performance. Successful CPSD programs must also recognize that poverty is not a one-size-fits-all phenomenon. While some Canadians experience long-term poverty, others move out of poverty after a relatively short period. This has considerable implications for the planning and development of CPSD programs. The social and economic difficulties faced by people with inadequate income year after year are different from those experienced by people who are poor for a year or two. An effective CPSD program must address the different needs of these two groups. Finally, successful CPSD programs must also challenge the stigma and blame society has traditionally placed on those living in poverty.

| "Children don't naturally kill. It is a learned skill. And they learn it from . . . violence as entertainment in television, the movies, and interactive video games."

VIOLENCE IN THE MEDIA CAUSES JUVENILE CRIME

Dave Grossman

In the following viewpoint, Dave Grossman argues that violent images on television, in movies, and in video games are responsible for the increase in the violent crime rate. He contends that children who grow up watching violence learn to associate it with pleasurable activities and so lose their innate aversion toward killing humans. He concludes that parents and children both need to learn that violence—in the media and in real life— is not fun and is not a game. Grossman, a psychology instructor and retired Army lieutenant colonel, is the director of the Killology Research Group, an organization that studies the psychology of killing, in Jonesboro, Arkansas. He is also the author of On Killing: The Psychological Cost of Learning to Kill in War and Society.

As you read, consider the following questions:

1. According to a study cited by Grossman, what percentage of soldiers actually fired their guns at enemy soldiers during World War II?
2. How did the U.S. military overcome the typical soldier's aversion to shooting at enemy soldiers, according to the author?
3. What are three methods cited by the author that are used to increase the kill rate of soldiers?

Excerpted from Dave Grossman, "Trained to Kill," Christianity Today, August 10, 1998. Reprinted with permission.

I am from Jonesboro, Arkansas. I travel the world training medical, law enforcement, and U.S. military personnel about the realities of warfare. I try to make those who carry deadly force keenly aware of the magnitude of killing. Too many law enforcement and military personnel act like "cowboys," never stopping to think about who they are and what they are called to do. I hope I am able to give them a reality check.

So here I am, a world traveler and an expert in the field of "killology," and the largest school massacre in American history happens in my hometown of Jonesboro, Arkansas. That was the March 24, 1998, schoolyard shooting deaths of four girls and a teacher. Ten others were injured, and two boys, ages 11 and 13, are in jail, charged with murder. [The two boys were remanded to a juvenile detention center until their eighteenth birthday.] . . .

KILLING IS UNNATURAL

Before retiring from the military, I spent almost a quarter of a century as an army infantry officer and a psychologist, learning and studying how to enable people to kill. Believe me, we are very good at it. But it does not come naturally; you have to be taught to kill. And just as the army is conditioning people to kill, we are indiscriminately doing the same thing to our children, but without the safeguards.

After the Jonesboro killings, the head of the American Academy of Pediatrics Task Force on Juvenile Violence came to town and said that children don't naturally kill. It is a learned skill. And they learn it from abuse and violence in the home and, most pervasively, from violence as entertainment in television, the movies, and interactive video games.

Killing requires training because there is a built-in aversion to killing one's own kind. I can best illustrate this from drawing on my own work in studying killing in the military. . . .

Throughout human history, when humans fight each other, there is a lot of posturing. Adversaries make loud noises and puff themselves up, trying to daunt the enemy. There is a lot of fleeing and submission. Ancient battles were nothing more than great shoving matches. It was not until one side turned and ran that most of the killing happened, and most of that was stabbing people in the back. All of the ancient military historians report that the vast majority of killing happened in pursuit when one side was fleeing. . . .

During World War II, U.S. Army Brig. Gen. S.L.A. Marshall had a team of researchers study what soldiers did in battle. For the first time in history, they asked individual soldiers what they did in battle. They discovered that only 15 to 20 percent of the individual riflemen could bring themselves to fire at an exposed enemy soldier.

That is the reality of the battlefield. Only a small percentage of soldiers are able and willing to participate. Men are willing to die, they are willing to sacrifice themselves for their nation; but they are not willing to kill. It is a phenomenal insight into human nature; but when the military became aware of that, they systematically went about the process of trying to fix this "problem." From the military perspective, a 15 percent firing rate among riflemen is like a 15 percent literacy rate among librarians. And fix it the military did. By the Korean War, around 55 percent of the soldiers were willing to fire to kill. And by Vietnam, the rate rose to over 90 percent.

DESENSITIZATION

How the military increases the killing rate of soldiers in combat is instructive, because our culture today is doing the same thing to our children. The training methods militaries use are brutalization, classical conditioning, operant conditioning, and role modeling. I will explain these in the military context and show how these same factors are contributing to the phenomenal increase of violence in our culture.

Brutalization and desensitization are what happens at boot camp. From the moment you step off the bus you are physically and verbally abused: countless pushups, endless hours at attention or running with heavy loads, while carefully trained professionals take turns screaming at you. Your head is shaved, you are herded together naked and dressed alike, losing all individuality. This brutalization is designed to break down your existing mores and norms and to accept a new set of values that embrace destruction, violence, and death as a way of life. In the end, you are desensitized to violence and accept it as a normal and essential survival skill in your brutal new world.

Something very similar to this desensitization toward violence is happening to our children through violence in the media—but instead of 18-year-olds, it begins at the age of 18 months when a child is first able to discern what is happening on television. At that age, a child can watch something happening on television and mimic that action. But it isn't until children are six or seven years old that the part of the brain kicks in that lets them understand where information comes from. Even though young children have some understanding of what it means to pretend, they are developmentally unable to distinguish clearly between fantasy and reality.

When young children see somebody shot, stabbed, raped, brutalized, degraded, or murdered on TV, to them it is as though it were actually happening. To have a child of three, four, or five watch a "splatter" movie, learning to relate to a character for the first 90 minutes and then in the last 30 minutes watch helplessly as that new friend is hunted and brutally murdered is the moral and psychological equivalent of introducing your child to a friend, letting her play with that friend, and then butchering that friend in front of your child's eyes. And this happens to our children hundreds upon hundreds of times.

AGGRAVATED ASSAULT RATES

The per capita murder rate doubled in the United States between 1957—when the FBI started keeping track of the data—and 1992. A fuller picture of the problem, however, is indicated by the rate people are *attempting* to kill one another—the aggravated assault rate. That rate in America has gone from around 60 per 100,000 in 1957 to over 440 per 100,000 by the mid-1990s.

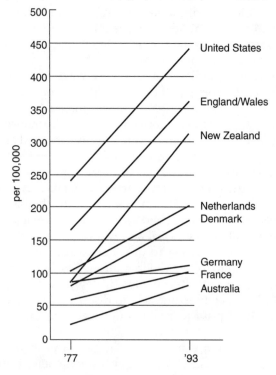

Dave Grossman, *Christianity Today*, August 10, 1998.

Sure, they are told: "Hey, it's all for fun. Look, this isn't real, it's just TV." And they nod their little heads and say *okay*. But they can't tell the difference. Can you remember a point in your life or in your children's lives when dreams, reality, and television were all jumbled together? That's what it is like to be at that level of psychological development. That's what the media are doing to them.

The *Journal of the American Medical Association* published the definitive epidemiological study on the impact of TV violence. The research demonstrated what happened in numerous nations after television made its appearance as compared to nations and regions without TV. The two nations or regions being compared are demographically and ethnically identical; only one variable is different: the presence of television. In every nation, region, or city with television, there is an immediate explosion of violence on the playground, and within 15 years there is a doubling of the murder rate. Why 15 years? That is how long it takes for the brutalization of a three- to five-year-old to reach the "prime crime age." That is how long it takes for you to reap what you have sown when you brutalize and desensitize a three-year-old.

Today the data linking violence in the media to violence in society are superior to those linking cancer and tobacco. Hundreds of sound scientific studies demonstrate the social impact of brutalization by the media. The *Journal of the American Medical Association* concluded that "the introduction of television in the 1950's caused a subsequent doubling of the homicide rate, i.e., long-term childhood exposure to television is a causal factor behind approximately one half of the homicides committed in the United States, or approximately 10,000 homicides annually." The article went on to say that ". . . if, hypothetically, television technology had never been developed, there would today be 10,000 fewer homicides each year in the United States, 70,000 fewer rapes, and 700,000 fewer injurious assaults."

CLASSICAL CONDITIONING

Classical conditioning is like the famous case of Pavlov's dogs you learned about in Psychology 101: The dogs learned to associate the ringing of the bell with food, and, once conditioned, the dogs could not hear the bell without salivating. . . .

What is happening to our children is the reverse of the aversion therapy portrayed in the movie *A Clockwork Orange*. In *A Clockwork Orange*, a brutal sociopath, a mass murderer, is strapped to a chair and forced to watch violent movies while he is injected with a drug that nauseates him. So he sits and gags and retches as he watches the movies. After hundreds of repetitions of this, he associates violence with nausea, and it limits his ability to be violent.

We are doing the exact opposite: Our children watch vivid pictures of human suffering and death, and they learn to associate it with their favorite soft drink and candy bar, or their girlfriend's perfume.

After the Jonesboro shootings, one of the high-school teachers told me how her students reacted when she told them about the shootings at the middle school. "They laughed," she told me with dismay. A similar reaction happens all the time in movie theaters when there is bloody violence. The young people laugh and cheer and keep right on eating popcorn and drinking pop. We have raised a generation of barbarians who have learned to associate violence with pleasure, like the Romans cheering and snacking as the Christians were slaughtered in the Colosseum.

The result is a phenomenon that functions much like AIDS, which I call AVIDS—Acquired Violence Immune Deficiency Syndrome. AIDS has never killed anybody. It destroys your immune system, and then other diseases that shouldn't kill you become fatal. Television violence by itself does not kill you. It destroys your violence immune system and conditions you to derive pleasure from violence. And once you are at close range with another human being, and it's time for you to pull that trigger, Acquired Violence Immune Deficiency Syndrome can destroy your midbrain resistance.

OPERANT CONDITIONING

The third method the military uses is operant conditioning, a very powerful procedure of stimulus-response, stimulus-response. A benign example is the use of flight simulators to train pilots. An airline pilot in training sits in front of a flight simulator for endless hours; when a particular warning light goes on, he is taught to react in a certain way. When another warning light goes on, a different reaction is required. Stimulus-response, stimulus-response, stimulus-response. One day the pilot is actually flying a jumbo jet; the plane is going down, and 300 people are screaming behind him. He is wetting his seat cushion, and he is scared out of his wits; but he does the right thing. Why? Because he has been conditioned to respond reflexively to this particular crisis.

When people are frightened or angry, they will do what they have been conditioned to do. In fire drills, children learn to file out of the school in orderly fashion. One day there is a real fire, and they are frightened out of their wits; but they do exactly what they have been conditioned to do, and it saves their lives.

The military and law-enforcement community have made killing a conditioned response. This has substantially raised the firing rate on the modern battlefield. Whereas infantry training in World War II used bull's-eye targets, now soldiers learn to fire at realistic, man-shaped silhouettes that pop into their field of view. That is the stimulus. The trainees have only a split second to engage the target. The conditioned response is to shoot the target, and then it drops. Stimulus-response, stimulus-response, stimulus-response—soldiers or police officers experience hundreds of repetitions. Later, when soldiers are on the battlefield or a police officer is walking a beat and somebody pops up with a gun, they will shoot reflexively and shoot to kill. We know that 75 to 80 percent of the shooting on the modern battlefield is the result of this kind of stimulus-response training.

Now, if you're a little troubled by that, how much more should we be troubled by the fact that every time a child plays an interactive point-and-shoot video game, he is learning the exact same conditioned reflex and motor skills.

I was an expert witness in a murder case in South Carolina offering mitigation for a kid who was facing the death penalty. I tried to explain to the jury that interactive video games had conditioned him to shoot a gun to kill. He had spent hundreds of dollars on video games learning to point and shoot, point and shoot. One day he and his buddy decided it would be fun to rob the local convenience store. They walked in, and he pointed a snub-nosed .38 pistol at the clerk's head. The clerk turned to look at him, and the defendant shot reflexively from about six feet. The bullet hit the clerk right between the eyes—which is a pretty remarkable shot with that weapon at that range—and killed this father of two. Afterward, we asked the boy what happened and why he did it. It clearly was not part of the plan to kill the guy—it was being videotaped from six different directions. He said, "I don't know. It was a mistake. It wasn't supposed to happen."

ROLE MODELS

In the military and law-enforcement worlds, the right option is often not to shoot. But you never, never put your quarter in that video machine with the intention of not shooting. There is always some stimulus that sets you off. And when he was excited, and his heart rate went up, and vasoconstriction closed his forebrain down, this young man did exactly what he was conditioned to do: he reflexively pulled the trigger, shooting accurately just like all those times he played video games.

This process is extraordinarily powerful and frightening. The result is ever more homemade pseudosociopaths who kill reflexively and show no remorse. Our children are learning to kill and learning to like it; and then we have the audacity to say, "Oh my goodness, what's wrong?"

One of the boys allegedly involved in the Jonesboro shootings (and they are just boys) had a fair amount of experience shooting real guns. The other one was a nonshooter and, to the best of our knowledge, had almost no experience shooting. Between them, those two boys fired 27 shots from a range of over 100 yards, and they hit 15 people. That's pretty remarkable shooting. We run into these situations often—kids who have never picked up a gun in their lives pick up a real gun and are incredibly accurate. Why? Video games. . . .

FIGHTING BACK

We ought to work toward legislation that outlaws violent video games for children. There is no constitutional right for a child to play an interactive video game that teaches him weapons-handling skills or that simulates destruction of God's creatures.

The day may also be coming when we are able to seat juries in America who are willing to sock it to the networks in the only place they really understand—their wallets. After the Jonesboro shootings, Time magazine said: "As for media violence, the debate there is fast approaching the same point that discussions about the health impact of tobacco reached some time ago—it's over. Few researchers bother any longer to dispute that bloodshed on TV and in the movies has an effect on kids who witness it."

Most of all, the American people need to learn the lesson of Jonesboro: Violence is not a game; it's not fun, it's not something that we do for entertainment. Violence kills.

| "Blaming media [for teenage
violence] is merely the simplest,
most expedient way to explain what
can't be explained."

VIOLENCE IN THE MEDIA DOES NOT CAUSE JUVENILE CRIME

Jon Katz

In the following viewpoint, author and media critic Jon Katz contends that the spate of schoolyard killings is not due to violence in the media but to the ease at which juveniles can obtain guns. Although the media has broadcast increasingly violent imagery, the rate of juvenile crime has been dropping for years, he maintains. Ultimately, the blame for these tragedies lies with the gun lobby that makes it easy for children to obtain guns, he argues.

As you read, consider the following questions:

1. How do the media contribute to the illusion that the media and entertainment industry are responsible for violence, in the author's opinion?
2. How many people were killed and wounded in school shootings in 1998, according to Katz?
3. How many children are abused by their families as opposed to children who are abused by someone they met over the Internet, as cited by Katz?

From the president on down, most of our voluble moral guardians are nowhere to be seen when kids like Kipland Kinkel get hold of lethal weapons in heartland America and cut down innocent people for no discernible reason. [Kinkel shot and killed his parents and then killed two students and wounded nineteen others at his Oregon school in May 1998.]

EMOTIONALLY DISTURBED PEOPLE WITH GUNS

As every months' headlines make clearer, the worst violence in modern American life cannot be blamed on rappers or on Hollywood producers. These crimes are committed by emotionally disturbed people—LA freeway shooters to AK-47-toting postal workers to troubled teenage boys—with nearly unrestricted access to deadly devices.

Horrific scenes of unprovoked, random, and incomprehensible slaughter have become an American ritual. Provoked by some small or even imagined slight—a break-up, a firing, a denied promotion, a look—the troubled man or boy gets a gun and shoots as many people as he can. Sometimes he is overwhelmed or caught; sometimes he kills himself first.

The police rarely manage to get to the workplace or schoolyard or mall in time, leaving victims and their families condemned to a particular contemporary hell. They not only see the people they love get murdered or maimed, but since the rampage seldom has a real reason behind it, they can never experience resolution or comprehension, let alone any kind of justice.

In fact, because the killers increasingly are children, even the recourse of that other American rite, the vengeance of the death penalty, is not an option—although blood-thirsty legislatures are already working to change that.

Why is it that William Bennett, the media's anointed Morals Czar and the self-appointed protector of children's values, isn't on TV expressing outrage at the ease with which kids can get pistols, rifles, and assault guns? Where's Bob Dole, who campaigned for the presidency by decrying violent imagery from Hollywood? Why the silence from Senator Joseph Lieberman of Connecticut, who calls regular press conferences to denounce the violence on Jerry Springer's talk show? And from Senator James Exon of Alaska, who labored to protect America's young by conceiving the Communications Decency Act? Why condolences from Bill Clinton, but no drafts of bills and proposals to control the sale and movement of guns whose only purpose is to kill people?

Children have been exploited for decades not only by sexual

predators but by politicians eager to capitalize on their parents' fears about new information technologies and popular culture. As a result, most Americans believe media is responsible for violence, a notion ironically advanced by the very same media's own inept and distorted reporting about violence and the young.

Many parents believe that TV bears primary responsibility for violence, that the Internet is awash with dangerous perverts, and that movies, videogames, and VCRs have rotted the brains and the values of the weak-minded young, infecting them with a predilection for mayhem.

The manipulable media have been all too happy to disseminate such fears. Objectivity, a cherished journalistic principle, permits reporters to pass along other people's opinions rather than trouble themselves to find out where the truth lies.

VIOLENCE

So most Americans really don't grasp that violence among the young has been dropping for years and that the primary users of new media technologies—the American middle-class young—are the safest group of children on the planet.

In 1998, Kipland Kinkel—plus his fellow disturbed teenage killers in other states—have killed and injured more children than have been killed by the Internet in its entire history. Their toll is far higher than that which can demonstrably be attributed to all the so-called dangerous imagery on television or in the movies.

According to federal statistics, no school shootings occurred in 1994; in 1997, there were four. In 1998, an 11-year-old boy and his 13-year-old friend were charged with killing four students and a teacher and wounding 10 others in Jonesboro, Arkansas. A high-school senior shot and killed a student in a school parking lot in Fayetteville, Tennessee. In Edinboro, Pennsylvania, a 14-year-old boy is accused of killing a teacher and wounding two students and another teacher at an eighth-grade graduation. Two days later, a 15-year-old girl was shot in the leg in a suburban Houston high-school classroom. In Washington, a 15-year-old boy got off his school bus carrying a gun and went home and shot himself in the head.

Although experts and sociologists have crammed TV talk shows to offer various theories about the contagion of teenage violence, it is clear that no one understands why these incidents occur. Blaming media is merely the simplest, most expedient way to explain what can't be explained.

In the midst of the Information Revolution, we are, as usual, on our own. Irresponsible and inaccurate posturing about violence and technology is epidemic. "What do you expect?" a New York City anchor angrily asked his deskmate during the late news the night of the Oregon killings. "All this violence on the Internet, on TV?" His co-anchor shook her head sympathetically and clucked, "Isn't that the sad truth!"

Are facts all that hard to come by?

CHILD ABUSE

Every day, writes Don Tapscott in *Growing Up Digital*, three children in the United States are murdered or die as a result of injuries inflicted by their parents or caretakers. Of the annual 3 million reported cases of child abuse, 127,000 cases involve child abandonment. Yet from March 1996 to March 1997, the National Center for Missing and Exploited Children recorded 23 cases related to the Internet. Ten involved the transfer of pornography, an adult soliciting sexual favors from minors, or sexual contact initiated over the Net—all despicable and intolerable episodes. Of the remaining 13 cases, two involved police officers posing as children, in two others the girls had previous histories as runaways. Nine others involved children over age 16 running away from home, purportedly to meet online acquaintances.

What these statistics indicate, Tapscott says, is that "children are 300,000 times more likely to be abused by one of their own relatives than by someone they have met over the Internet."

AN UNCONVINCING ARGUMENT

Sissella Bok, whose book *Mayhem* examines the effects of violence in media, writes that young people's lives are saturated with graphic violence in a way that's different and more dangerous than in previous generations.

"We have movie role models showing violence as fun, and videogames where you kill, and get rewarded for killing, for hours and hours." It is, she wrote, a "very combustible mix, enraged young people with access to semiautomatic weapons, exposed to violence as entertainment, violence shown as exciting and thrilling."

Unquestionably, the young grow up in an environment in which images of graphic violence are ubiquitous. But such arguments seem facile, unconvincing—maybe it's that "access to semiautomatic weapons" more than the rage or the games that's different from previous eras. If Bok's right, why do FBI statistics show violence among the young plummeting to its lowest levels since Prohibition, while violent imagery in media has indeed been increasing, along with cable programming and usage, movie attendance, and the advent of the Net?

And that's only one of the questions we need to be asking. Some others:

Why are almost all these killers male?

GUNS GUNS GUNS EASY TO GET TO USE

SO EASY A CHILD CAN OPERATE

GUN CONTROLS? AFTER ALL, ONLY 13,200 PEOPLE IN THE U.S. WERE KILLED BY GUNFIRE IN A YEAR

Copyright 1998 by Herblock in *The Washington Post*. Reprinted with permission.

Why do so many of these school shootings occur not in media-saturated urban areas but in rural heartland communities, generally thought more conservative and traditional? Is there a connection to the rural popularity of hunting, as in Springfield?

GUNS ARE EASILY OBTAINED

The media habits of these teenage suspects aren't yet clear. The common denominator linking them, to date, is quite clear: They can easily find guns. Why haven't journalists and politicians focused on this as the most pressing issue connecting these tragedies, a far more convincing common denominator than violence on TV?

We all know the answer. Because the gun lobby is too powerful, and because journalists can hide behind the comfortable ethos of objectivity, which makes avoiding the truth not only excusable but virtuous. All they have to do is make sure to quote everybody else's stalemating opinions.

When it comes to the sale and distribution of rapid-fire assault weapons, the gun lobby is our modern equivalent of Murder Inc., responsible for vast tragedy and suffering. That this is so obviously, irrefutably true, even when it comes to stopping the slaughter of helpless children, is a bloody indictment of both journalism and politics, two of our most cowardly and morally bankrupt contemporary public institutions.

PERIODICAL BIBLIOGRAPHY

The following articles have been selected to supplement the diverse views presented in this chapter. Addresses are provided for periodicals not indexed in the *Readers' Guide to Periodical Literature*, the *Alternative Press Index*, the *Social Sciences Index*, or the *Index to Legal Periodicals and Books*.

Robert James Bidinotto — "The 'Root Causes' of Crime," *Freeman*, June 1995. Available from Foundation for Economic Education, Irvington-on-Hudson, NY 10533.

Canada and the World Backgrounder — "What Makes Criminals Tick?" December 1996.

Lisa Conyers and Philip D. Harvey — "Religion and Crime: Do They Go Together?" *Free Inquiry*, Summer 1996. Available from 1310 Sweet Home Rd., Amherst, NY 14228.

John J. DiIulio Jr. — "The Coming of the Super-Predators," *Weekly Standard*, November 27, 1995. Available from 1211 Avenue of the Americas, New York, NY 10036.

Patrick Fagan — "The Real Root Cause of Violent Crime," *Vital Speeches of the Day*, December 15, 1995.

Jan Farrington — "When Violence Comes to School," *Current Health*, April/May 1998.

James K. Fitzpatrick — "Can Teenagers Survive Marilyn Manson?" *New Oxford Review*, November 1997. Available from 1069 Kains Ave., Berkeley, CA 94706.

Jib Fowles — "The Violence Against Television Violence," *Television Quarterly*, vol. 28, no. 1, 1996.

Joe Klein — "When Work Disappears: The World of the New Urban Poor," *New Republic*, October 28, 1996.

Salim Muwakkil — "Rap's Dilemma," *In These Times*, March 8, 1998.

Dorothy Nelkin — "Biology Is Not Destiny," *New York Times*, September 28, 1995.

Tabitha M. Powledge — "Genetics and the Control of Crime," *BioScience*, January 1996.

Adolph Reed — "Dissing the Underclass," *Progressive*, December 1996.

Byron M. Roth — "Crime and Child-Rearing," *Society*, November/December 1996.

Jim Wilson — "The Chemistry of Violence," *Popular Mechanics*, April 1998.

DOES CONTROLLING GUNS CONTROL CRIME?

Chapter Preface

Opponents of gun control have long argued that any restrictions on the purchasing and use of guns to prevent criminals from obtaining the weapons would be ineffective. Criminals steal their guns, they maintain, not buy them. Therefore, the gun rights advocates assert, gun control regulations merely restrict the rights of legal buyers who want to exercise their Second Amendment rights.

A study released late in 1998 using data from the Bureau of Alcohol, Tobacco, and Firearms appears to refute that argument, however. The study traced the origins of guns that were used in homicides and other crimes and found that 20 percent of them had been purchased from a federally licensed gun dealer within one week of the murder. Furthermore, nearly half of the guns traced had been purchased from a dealer within three years of the commission of a crime. Gun control supporters maintain that these results show that guns are moving from manufacturer to dealer to criminal much faster than was previously believed. The advocates also contend that manufacturers, distributors, and dealers know of this illegal flow of weapons to criminals and do nothing to stop it.

Gun rights supporters and the firearms industry deny the charge. They point to surveys that show that almost 500,000 guns are stolen each year, 80 percent of which are taken from private homes. The advocates also claim that statistics purporting to show that guns are used to commit a crime shortly after being sold from a dealer are meaningless. "Obviously if a gun is stolen, it can be stolen when it is young, so their assumption is incorrect, that short 'time to crime' means the gun is purchased by a criminal and not stolen," asserts lawyer James P. Dorr.

In the following chapter, supporters of gun control and gun rights debate whether more guns mean more or less crime and whether gun control measures are effective at keeping the firearms out of the hands of criminals.

"Eliminating handguns would not eliminate rage or conflict but certainly would lower the life-threatening consequences of these encounters."

GUN CONTROL LAWS REDUCE CRIME

Richard Harwood

In the following viewpoint, Richard Harwood reports on a study that found that although crime rates in the United States are similar to the crime rates in other Western countries, the murder rate in the United States is much higher. The study's authors contend that the easy availability of guns accounts for the higher murder rates. Encounters between victim and victimizer can quickly turn deadly when a gun is handy, Harwood asserts. Harwood is a syndicated columnist.

As you read, consider the following questions:

1. How many Americans have been murdered since 1980, according to Harwood?
2. What is the homicide rate per 100,000 people in the United States, as cited by the author?
3. How does murder affect society, according to Harwood?

Reprinted from Richard Harwood, "America's Unchecked Epidemic," *The Washington Post National Weekly Edition*, December 8, 1997, with permission. Copyright © The Washington Post Company.

A mericans have invested a great deal of wealth and effort in this century to keep death at bay, and they have had a lot of success. Cholera, smallpox, typhoid have been eliminated in this country. Other diseases that once killed millions now are cured easily or prevented. The average American's life span has been extended by nearly 30 years.

Health and medical care have become our leading industry. We spend more on these services than we spend for food, housing, automobiles, clothes or education.

THE VIOLENCE EPIDEMIC

But neither money nor science has brought us any closer to solving or even moderating one epidemic in American life: violence. For at least a century and probably longer we have been the most murderous "developed" society on earth. Since 1980 nearly 400,000 Americans have died at the hands of fellow citizens—more than the number of Americans who died on the battlefields of World War I and World War II combined. It would take eight Vietnams to fill as many graves.

Our propensity to violence cannot be explained by the cliche that America is a uniquely "lawless" society. Franklin Zimring and Gordon Hawkins of the University of California write: "The reported rates [per 100,000 people] of both violent and nonviolent crime in the United States . . . are quite close to those found in countries like Australia, Canada and New Zealand." The rate of criminal assault is higher in those countries than here. In robberies, the United States is second to Poland and similar in rate to Italy, Australia, Czechoslovakia, Canada and England. Scandinavian robbery rates are not strikingly lower than those in this country. A study in 1992 revealed that London had a higher overall crime rate than New York City, including 66 percent more thefts and 57 percent more burglaries. But New York has 11 times as many murders.

So it is not crime that sets us apart. We have no more pickpockets, shoplifters, burglars, robbers or brawlers than Western Europe or the British Isles. But we have a surplus of killers—a large surplus. Our homicide rate is 20 times the rate in England and Wales, 10 times the rate in France and Germany and is exceeded only by a few Latin American countries, notably Colombia, Mexico and Brazil.

Why this is so is a mystery to medical scientists (psychiatrists and psychologists included) and to anthropologists and social scientists as well. Politicians have no answers. They wage futile "wars" on crime, expand the police forces and the offenses punishable by death keep a million citizens in prison, beef up law enforcement agencies and equip them with everything from tanks to helicopter gunships. Through it all, the homicide rate remains almost constant—roughly eight to 10 murders for every 100,000 people in the course of a year.

A SERIOUS PROBLEM

When 20,000 to 25,000 people are being murdered every year, you've got a problem. It's not a huge problem in the context of death in America; more than 2.25 million of us die every year from all causes—including 30,000 to 40,000 from AIDS, 40,000 or so in automobile accidents and about 30,000 as a result of suicide.

But even in that context, murder is a serious problem. It poisons society with fear and suspicion, turns large areas of our cities into combat zones and contributes to urban flight.

FEWER GUNS EQUALS LESS CRIME

Face the fact that easy access to guns is one of the biggest factors in violent crime. Then support law enforcement's efforts to get Saturday Night Specials off the market, restrict multiple purchases of guns and allow the police some discretion in issuing permits to concealed weapons. After the Brady bill and assault weapons ban were enacted in 1994, the number of murders committed with firearms fell by 11.6 percent the following year. The number of officers killed by assault weapons was reduced from 10 in 1995 to one in 1996.

William J. Bratton, *New York Times*, June 20, 1998.

Still, despite our cowboy image in much of the world, it is irrational to assume that a propensity for murder is rampant in the American character; 99.99 percent of us never murder anyone. And there is no uniformity among those who do. Some regions have more violent traditions than others, the South in particular: Louisiana's murder rate today is 20 times the rate in Vermont. Men are more murderous than women. Cities have proportionately more murders than suburbs and rural areas. The 20 largest U.S. cities have 11.5 percent of the American population but account for 34 percent of the reported homicides. African Americans, heavily concentrated in these cities, are at far more risk of death by homicide than nonblacks. They are 13 percent of the American population, but they account for 45 percent of homicide victims and 55 percent of suspects charged with homicide, according to calculations by Zimring and Hawkins. Many theories are offered to explain the relatively high level of lethal violence in these urban communities, but none has been validated. Whatever the "causal" factors, the number and percentage of blacks charged with homicide in the age groups most prone to violence—15 to 34—is tiny, roughly a tenth of one percent. And if black homicides were ignored in the calculations, the U.S. homicide rate still would be three to five times greater than the rates in Europe and Britain.

AN ARSENAL OF GUNS

Zimring and Hawkins conclude that the one "causal" factor that sets us apart from the rest of the world is the huge arsenal of handguns—estimated at from 50 million to 70 million—that makes it possible to settle with finality the passionate domestic arguments and street disputes that produce most of our homicides. Eliminating handguns would not eliminate rage or conflict but certainly would lower the life-threatening consequences of these encounters.

People will argue that other deadly weapons—knives, blunt instruments, poison and the noose will remain available to people who want to kill. Sure. They're available all over the world, too, but nowhere else is murder so commonplace.

It would take political courage to do anything about the gun problem, and it is in short supply in Washington. But no other remedy—medical, chemical, technological or spiritual—is at hand or even on the horizon.

| "Gun control runs aground on this simple fact: people who would use guns to break laws would also break laws to use guns."

GUN CONTROL LAWS DO NOT REDUCE CRIME

Sheldon Richman

In the following viewpoint, Sheldon Richman argues that gun control is ineffective at preventing crime. Richman asserts that even if criminals are prevented from buying guns at gun shops, they may obtain them through burglary or the black market. Furthermore, if law-abiding citizens are prevented from acquiring or keeping their guns due to gun control laws, they will be unable to protect themselves and others against criminals who still have their firearms, he maintains. Therefore, Richman concludes, gun control does not make the world safer. Richman is the editor of *Freeman* magazine, a monthly libertarian journal.

As you read, consider the following questions:

1. According to Richman, what are the three unseen effects of gun control?
2. Why is the assertion that gun control will reduce the number of people killed by gunshots a fallacy, in Richman's view?
3. Why would a world without guns not be any safer than one in which lawful people were free to own them, according to the author?

Reprinted from Sheldon Richman, "The Seen and Unseen in Gun Control," *The Freeman*, October 1998, with permission.

The heinous shootings by young people at public schools around the country have predictably renewed calls for more gun control. Advocates of gun bans commit a classic fallacy that is usually associated with economic policy. But it fully applies to all government policy, including gun control.

In the nineteenth century, the French economist Frederic Bastiat explained that in order to understand the consequences of a policy, you must consider both "what is seen and what is unseen." This was also the "one lesson" taught by Bastiat's intellectual descendant, Henry Hazlitt, in his famous book *Economics in One Lesson*. Hazlitt identified the "persistent tendency of men to see only the immediate effects of a given policy, or its effects only on a special group, and to neglect to inquire what the long-run effects of that policy will be not only on that special group but on all groups. It is the fallacy of overlooking secondary consequences."

The famous case of neglecting the unseen, of course, is the broken shop window. Observers are likely to notice that a glass maker will have new income to spend. They miss that had the glass not been broken, the owner of the window could have spent his money to better his situation rather than merely to restore it. That's the unseen.

If you think this is a seldom-committed fallacy, just read the newspaper after the next hurricane or earthquake. Five'll get you ten that someone will herald the silver lining: reconstruction projects.

If we look at only obvious, primary consequences, we will badly misjudge circumstances and any resulting policy will be bad. That is one problem with gun control.

Unseen Gun Sales

Advocates of gun bans react to a shooting by saying that if the assailant had had no access to firearms, that shooting could not have occurred. Of course, that is true: the shooting required a gun. But this proves much less than the controllers think. It doesn't mean that had the killer not been able to get a gun legally, he couldn't have gotten one at all. Fans of the Brady law, which requires a waiting period and background check for gun buyers, rejoice that tens of thousands of people have had gun applications turned down. (Most were not violent criminals.) But that's not the end of the story. Will a thug who is turned away from a gun shop give up so easily? Or is he apt to go into the black market to buy a firearm? Worse, might he not break into a gun shop or someone's home to steal a gun?

Gun control runs aground on this simple fact: people who would use guns to break laws would also break laws to use guns.

The controllers see the turn-down at the gun counter. They don't see, and therefore they don't take account of, the alternative methods of acquiring firearms.

UNSEEN VICTIMS

The failure to look for the unseen does not stop there. After each mass shooting, we hear recited the statistics on how many people are murdered by gunshot each year. The implication is that without guns, the total murder rate would be reduced by that number. We are also reminded of how many accidental shootings occur (the firearms accident rate, however, has been falling), and are led to believe that if legal gun possession were severely restricted, fewer people would die each year from gunshots. Not true.

To be sure, some people who were killed might be alive today. But some who were *not* killed might have been. How so? It might come as a surprise, because it gets no publicity, but people use guns defensively (often without firing them) two and a half million times each year. As John Lott of the University of Chicago Law School points out, this number includes incidents in which mass shootings are prevented or curtailed and in which mothers thwart car-jackings when their children are in the cars.

Writes Lott in the July/August 1998 issue of the *American Enterprise*: "On the surface, [school shootings] seem to present a strong argument for restricting private gun ownership. But the truth is, guns wielded by private citizens have saved lives in such incidents, including some of the recent ones." He reminds us that the shooting spree at a Pearl, Mississippi, school in 1998 might have taken more victims had an assistant principal not retrieved a gun from his car and used it to hold the student assailant until the police appeared. A similar thing happened to end the student shooting incident at Edinboro, Pennsylvania.

The deaths that do *not* occur because lawful people have guns cannot be seen and therefore are not entered in the plus column of the ledger. If guns are banned, lawful people, not criminals, will be denied a key method of using force—in defense of self and others. Thus, more may die at the hands of criminals than do today.

We can demonstrate this negatively with a real incident. Some years ago, George Hennard, Jr., walked into Luby's Cafeteria in Killeen, Texas, and opened fire, killing 23 patrons and wounding

28 others. Suzanne Gratia Hupp was having lunch there with her parents and saw them murdered. It so happens that this woman usually carried a handgun in her purse (which at the time was illegal to do). But on this day, fearing revocation of a recently received occupational license, she left the gun in her car when she and her parents went into the cafeteria. She is convinced that if she had taken the gun with her, she would have stopped the shooter. Her parents, and others, might have been spared. They can be counted among the victims of gun control.

Concealed Carry

There is still another kind of "unseen" in the issue of gun control. A majority of states has now legalized the concealed carry of handguns for citizens who satisfy a few objective criteria. Formerly, local authorities had wide discretion in granting such permits. Where concealed carry is allowed, it is the criminals who are plagued by the unseen. They can't know who has a gun and who doesn't. This creates a free-rider problem—for the thugs. People who choose not to carry firearms nevertheless benefit from the fact that others may and do carry them. Criminals don't typically like to attack dangerous targets. Since criminals can't know in advance who's carrying and who isn't carrying a gun, they have to assume anyone might be—if not the potential victim, then someone nearby. That's how to create safety on the streets.

A world without any guns would not be safer than one in which lawful people were free to own them. Without guns, bigger, stronger thugs would have an advantage over smaller, weaker victims. Women, especially, would suffer. In that world, the unseen would be the victims of fatal beatings and stabbings who would have remained alive had they possessed firearms with which to defend themselves.

"Only one policy was found to reduce deaths and injuries from [multiple-victim public] shootings: allowing law-abiding citizens to carry concealed handguns."

CARRYING CONCEALED WEAPONS PREVENTS CRIME

John R. Lott Jr.

Laws that restrict gun ownership do not reduce gun violence, argues John R. Lott Jr. in the following viewpoint, but actually prevent law-abiding citizens from protecting themselves against crime and criminals. States that allow their residents to carry concealed weapons experienced a significant drop in violent crime rates, he maintains, because criminals are less likely to attack anyone if they think their potential victim may be armed. Therefore, Lott asserts, the best way to reduce gun violence is to allow law-abiding citizens to carry concealed weapons. Lott is the John M. Olin law and economics professor at the University of Chicago School of Law and the author of More Guns, Less Crime: Understanding Crime and Gun Control.

As you read, consider the following questions:

1. Who obeys gun-control laws, according to Lott?
2. How many multiple-victim public shootings did the United States average each year between 1977 and 1995, as cited by the author?
3. By what percentage did multiple-victim public shootings decline when states allowed law-abiding citizens to carry concealed weapons, according to Lott?

Reprinted from John R. Lott Jr., "How to Stop Mass Public Shootings," Los Angeles Times, May 25, 1998, with permission.

It is too bad Barbra Streisand won't debate Charlton Heston over the meaning of the 2nd Amendment. Yet, as entertaining as that debate would be, the more important question is: Would gun control have prevented the horrific shootings discussed in her movie based on Colin Ferguson's rampage, which took six lives on the Long Island Railroad in 1993?

In Streisand's movie, *The Long Island Incident*, the solution is clear: more regulations of guns. However, what might appear to be the most obvious policy may actually cost lives. When gun-control laws are passed, it is law-abiding citizens, not would-be criminals, who adhere to them. Police officers or armed guards cannot be stationed everywhere, so gun-control laws risk creating situations in which the good guys cannot defend themselves.

CARRYING WEAPONS SAVES LIVES

Other countries have followed a different solution. Twenty or so years ago in Israel, there were many instances of terrorists pulling out machine guns and firing away at civilians in public. However, with expanded concealed-handgun use by Israeli citizens, terrorists soon found ordinary people pulling pistols on them. Suffice it to say, terrorists in Israel no longer engage in such public shootings.

The one recent shooting of schoolchildren in the Middle East further illustrates these points. On March 13, 1997, seven Israeli girls were shot to death by a Jordanian soldier while they visited Jordan's so-called Island of Peace. The *Los Angeles Times* reported that the Israelis had "complied with Jordanian requests to leave their weapons behind when they entered the border enclave. Otherwise, they might have been able to stop the shooting, several parents said."

Hardly mentioned in the massive news coverage of the school-related shootings in 1997 and 1998 is how they ended. Two of the four shootings were stopped by a citizen displaying a gun. In the October 1997 shooting spree at a high school in Pearl, Mississippi, which left two students dead, an assistant principal retrieved a gun from his car and physically immobilized the shooter while waiting for the police.

More recently, the school-related shooting in Edinboro, Pennsylvania, in April 1998, which left one teacher dead, was stopped only after a bystander pointed a shotgun at the shooter when he started to reload his gun. The police did not arrive for another 10 minutes.

Who knows how many lives were saved by these prompt responses?

Anecdotal stories are not sufficient to resolve this debate. Together with my colleague William Landes, I have compiled data on all the multiple-victim public shootings occurring in the U.S. from 1977 to 1995. Included were incidents where at least two people were killed or injured in a public place; to focus on the type of shooting seen in the Ferguson rampage, we excluded gang wars or shootings that were the byproduct of another crime, such as robbery. The U.S. averaged 21 such shootings annually, with an average of 1.8 people killed and 2.7 wounded in each one.

We examined a range of different gun laws, such as waiting periods as well as methods of deterrence, such as the death penalty. However, only one policy was found to reduce deaths and injuries from these shootings: allowing law-abiding citizens to carry concealed handguns.

A DRAMATIC EFFECT

The effect of "shall-issue" concealed handgun laws, which give adults the right to carry concealed handguns if they do not have a criminal record or a history of significant mental illness, was dramatic. Thirty-one states now have such laws. When states passed them during the 19 years we studied, the number of multiple-victim public shootings declined by 84%. Deaths from

these shootings plummeted on average by 90%, injuries by 82%. Higher arrest rates and increased use of the death penalty slightly reduced the incidence of these events, but we could not conclusively determine such an effect.

Unfortunately, much of the public policy debate is driven by lopsided coverage of gun use. Horrific events like the Colin Ferguson shooting receive massive news coverage, as they should, but the 2.5 million times each year that people use guns defensively—including cases in which public shootings are stopped before they happen—are ignored.

Concealed handgun laws also deter other crimes from occurring. I recently analyzed the FBI's crime data for all 3,054 counties in the United States from 1977 to 1994. The more people who obtained permits, the more violent crime declined. After concealed handgun laws have been in effect for 5 years, murders declined by at least 15%, rapes by 9% and robberies by 11%. Permit holders were found to be extremely law-abiding, and data on accidental deaths and suicides indicate that there were no increases.

The possibility of a law-abiding citizen carrying a concealed handgun is apparently enough to convince many would-be killers that they will not be successful. Without permitting law-abiding citizens the right to carry guns, we risk leaving victims as sitting ducks.

> "In most cases, a concealed weapon is useless as a means of protection. It tends to give carriers a false sense of security."

CARRYING CONCEALED WEAPONS DOES NOT PREVENT CRIME

Bill Kolender

Bill Kolender is the sheriff of San Diego County. In the following viewpoint, Kolender argues that a law that permits almost any resident to carry a concealed weapon is extremely dangerous. Studies have found that gun homicides increase in states that permit concealed weapons, he asserts. Furthermore, Kolender maintains that many people would use their guns to settle disputes in situations that normally would not turn violent, endangering the lives of law enforcement officers with each citizen they encounter.

As you read, consider the following questions:

1. To whom would the issuing authority be forced to issue concealed carry permits, in Kolender's opinion?
2. How many people are killed by guns in the United States each year, as cited by the author?
3. According to Kolender, what percentage of people are killed by people without criminal intent?

Excerpted from Bill Kolender, "Look for Trouble If Gun Law Is Eased," *San Diego Union-Tribune*, June 28, 1996, p. B11. Reprinted with permission.

W hen I hear about the efforts of the gun lobby to make it easier to get permits to carry concealed weapons in California, I immediately picture a Chargers-Raiders game . . . [with] its stands packed with gun-toting fans.

Proponents of this shocking scenario insist this would be the best and safest of all worlds. You couldn't pay me enough to be sitting in those stands. A football game or any public event teeming with armed individuals is a potential powder keg. An argument or a fist fight could escalate into a gun battle, and someone could get killed.

Law enforcement organizations throughout California vehemently oppose the weakening of requirements for carrying a concealed weapon. And polls show that nearly 75 percent of California voters are opposed as well. . . .

If [a bill legalizing the carrying of concealed weapons (CCW)] becomes law, nearly every California resident over the age of 21 will qualify to carry a concealed weapon as long as he or she has no record of a felony conviction or recorded history of mental illness. This bill removes the current requirement that an applicant show good and sufficient cause to be issued a permit.

The bill also eliminates the discretion of the issuing official. As the issuing agency for San Diego (California) County, the Sheriff's Office would be forced to parcel out permits to anyone meeting the minimum standards, including individuals convicted of assault, prowling or drunk driving. Felons who have plea bargained down to misdemeanor charges also would qualify for permits.

Don't get me wrong. I am not against the ownership of firearms. I recognize and understand the fear that drives some people to purchase guns. But I don't buy the argument that allowing average citizens to carry concealed handguns will cut down on crime and increase public safety.

In March 1995, a study by criminologists at the University of Maryland examined the effects of weakened concealed-weapons laws in Florida, Mississippi and Oregon, finding that gun homicides increased an average of 26 percent while other types of homicides stayed the same.

In most cases, a concealed weapon is useless as a means of protection. It tends to give carriers a false sense of security. Even police officers aren't entirely immune to gunshot wounds in confrontations with criminals. A 1993 FBI study shows that among 54 officers killed in 54 shooting incidents, 85 percent did not have a chance to fire their weapons. And 25 percent were shot with their own guns. Imagine, if these well-trained professionals cannot always protect themselves with their guns, how would the average citizen fare against an experienced criminal?

What few people realize is that the nation's 24,000 gun homicides each year don't rest on the shoulders of the violent criminal alone. Nearly 50 percent of murder victims are killed by people without criminal intent. The shouting match over a parking space, the fist fight on the playground or a lovers' quarrel can result in a death when guns are accessible.

More Guns Do Not Make Streets Safer

An analysis conducted by the Center to Prevent Handgun Violence, comparing the latest drop in crime rates among the states, provides compelling evidence that the gun lobby is wrong: more concealed handguns do not mean less crime. According to the Federal Bureau of Investigation's Uniform Crime Reports, from 1996 to 1997 the nation's overall crime rate dropped 3.2%, from 5086.6 to 4922.7 crimes per 100,000 population. More telling, crime fell faster in states that have strict carrying concealed weapons (CCW) laws or that don't allow the carrying of concealed weapons at all than in states which have lax CCW laws. This strongly suggests that, contrary to the arguments made by the National Rifle Association and others, states should not make it easier for citizens to carry concealed weapons in order to reduce crime.

Handgun Control, Inc., "Latest Crime Statistics Refute the Gun Lobby: More Guns on Our Streets Do Not Make Us Safer," January 18, 1999.

[A CCW law] also has the potential of raising the stakes for law enforcement officers—men and women on the front lines in the fight against violent crime. Our officers and deputies are already at risk due to the proliferation of handguns. [The law] would increase the potential hazard that police face in every traffic stop or any other encounter with a citizen.

And what message are we sending to our children when Mom or Dad comes home and tosses a gun on the kitchen table? Guns soon would come to represent the ultimate means of protection and even a status symbol for young people. Can we afford to send this message, particularly at a time when violent crime among juveniles is escalating?

If you share my concern that weakening concealed-weapons standards will lead to more crime, not less, please join me . . . in calling on our legislators. . . . Let them know you prefer civility and safety on our streets to fear, paranoia—and more guns.

VIEWPOINT

"Even though the ban [against
semiautomatic weapons] has been in
effect for only 14 months, ... there
has been a decrease in the use of
assault weapons in crimes."

BANNING SEMIAUTOMATIC RIFLES
REDUCES CRIME

Dianne Feinstein

In 1994, Congress passed the first ban on the manufacture and
sale of certain types of semiautomatic rifles, commonly known as
assault weapons. Dianne Feinstein argues in the following viewpoint that this ban has reduced gun violence. She contends that as
the availability of the assault weapons decreased, so, too, did the
number of people who were killed or injured by assault weapons
and the number of semiautomatic rifles that were used in crimes.
Feinstein maintains that the American public is very supportive of
the ban despite the efforts of the pro-gun lobby to repeal the assault weapons ban. Therefore, she argues, the gun ban should not
be repealed. Feinstein is a U.S. senator from California.

As you read, consider the following questions:

1. By what percentage did traces of assault weapons used in
   crimes decrease after the 1994 ban went into effect,
   according to Feinstein?
2. According to the author, what percentage of police officer
   gun deaths could be attributed to assault weapons in 1995
   after the ban went into effect?
3. How did the ban on assault weapons affect the supply and
   prices of the guns, as cited by Feinstein?

Reprinted from Dianne Feinstein, Symposium, "Is the Federal Ban on Assault Weapons
Working? Yes: The Weapons Are Harder to Get, and Police Fatalities Are Down," Insight,
February 26, 1996, by permission of Insight. Copyright ©1996 News World
Communications, Inc. All rights reserved.

Common sense tells one that no hunter or recreational sportsman should need a military-style assault weapon to shoot a deer, duck or clay pigeon. If they do, they might consider taking up bowling instead.

But after a hard-won ban on the manufacture and sale of these weapons was passed by Congress in 1994, the National Rifle Association, or NRA, and their stalwart supporters in the House and Senate want to repeal this legislation. The ban prohibits 19 types of semiautomatic weapons with high-capacity magazines. The NRA calls it "cosmetic" and repeatedly has said that it is not working.

Why, then, is the NRA working so feverishly to repeal it? The reason is that even though the ban has been in effect for only 14 months, there are signs it is, in fact, having an impact.

ASSAULT WEAPONS DEATHS DECLINE

Nationally, there has been a decrease in the use of assault weapons in crimes. The best information about the types of guns used in crimes can be found in police requests to the Bureau of Alcohol, Tobacco and Firearms, or ATF, to trace the sources of guns and where and when such weapons have been purchased. In 1993, the year before the ban went into effect, the 19 assault weapons banned by name under current law accounted for 8.2 percent of all ATF gun traces. The ban became effective on Sept. 13, 1994; from that date through November 1995, assault weapons composed only 4.3 percent of all gun traces—nearly a 50 percent decrease.

The use of such weapons to kill police officers also has declined. In 1994, when the ban was not in effect for most of the year, a study by Handgun Control Inc. found that assault weapons and guns with high-capacity magazines accounted for 41 percent of police gun deaths where the make and model of the weapon were known. In 1995, the figure fell to 28.6—a 30 percent decrease.

SUPPLY AND DEMAND

Perhaps most important is the impact of the ban on the availability of such weapons. Because the supply is decreasing, prices are going up. A survey conducted by my office yielded the following information for three of the most widely used assault weapons:

• A December 1993 issue of *Shotgun News* listed an SKS Paratrooper assault rifle for $99.95. The advertisement added, "This may be your last chance to buy at these prices!" The same weapon was offered in the November 1995 issue of the magazine for $129—a 30 percent increase—with the word **banned** in bold letters.

• *Shotgun News* offered the Norinco AK-47 for $695 in December 1993. By December 1995, the price had gone up to $850 and, according to the friendly clerk on the phone, only one remained for sale.

• In 1993, *Shotgun News* listed new Uzis for $795. By December 1995, the price was $995—a 25 percent increase.

Supplies are down. Prices are up. And they will continue to go up as these weapons become more and more difficult to find. The ban is working.

THE ATTEMPT TO REPEAL

Yet despite these very real gains in making assault weapons more difficult to obtain; despite the decline in the use of assault weapons against police officers and in all crimes; and despite sound reasoning and the will of 72 percent of the American people according to polls, opponents of the ban are determined to reverse course and repeal it.

Their relentless zeal is dumbfounding. Who besides drug dealers, gang members and revenge killers needs these weapons of war? Who do the politicians who are so willing to follow the NRA off a cliff like lemmings think they represent? Certainly not the public, who want these guns off the streets. Certainly not law-enforcement officers, who risk their lives against these weapons every day and strongly support the ban.

MILITARY WEAPONS ARE NOT HUNTING RIFLES

The import of assault weapons that use large-capacity military magazines should be banned. As everyone knows, you don't need an Uzi to go deer hunting. You don't need an AK-47 to go skeet shooting. These are military weapons, weapons of war. They were never meant for a day in the country, and they are certainly not meant for a night on the streets. Today we are working to make sure they stay off our streets.

Bill Clinton, Remarks on Assault Weapons, April 6, 1998.

A report released in January 1996 by the Center for Public Integrity provides a clue. Take Sen. Phil Gramm of Texas—a vocal opponent of the assault-weapons ban and a candidate for the 1996 Republican presidential nomination. The center's report, which tracked campaign contributions to various candidates, showed that the NRA is Gramm's biggest "lifetime patron," giving more than $440,000 to his political campaigns. The report also indicates that Gramm has not disappointed his benefactors, supporting the organization's interests on 18 major gun bills.

In 1995 I received a letter from a constituent, Carole Ann Taylor of Los Angeles, whose 17-year-old son, Willie, was killed by a shot in the back from an assault weapon. "After 17 years of loving, nurturing and guiding my only child, Willie, through birthday parties, Boy Scouts, basketball games, job interviews, Christmases and many other joy-filled events," she wrote, "someone with an accomplice—an AK-47—ended my son's life on a residential street as my son stood talking with a girlfriend on the sidewalk."

"I ask the 104th Congress," she continued, "was I in error to raise my son to live in a civilized society, or would military training for war have been more appropriate in sustaining his life? If, in fact, this is a civilized society, the assault weapon must remain on the ban list."

I couldn't agree more.

> "So-called 'assault weapons'. . .
> account for fewer than 1 percent of
> firearms recovered at crime scenes."

BANNING SEMIAUTOMATIC RIFLES WOULD NOT REDUCE CRIME

Joseph Perkins

In early 1998, Bill Clinton signed an executive order banning the importation of an additional 58 types of semiautomatic rifles into the United States. In the following viewpoint, Joseph Perkins contends that banning these weapons will not reduce crime rates. The imported "assault weapons" banned under the executive order are no different from semiautomatic weapons made in the United States, he maintains. The ban is simply part of an attempt to ban all semiautomatic weapons, he asserts. Perkins is an editorial writer for the *San Diego* (California) *Union-Tribune*.

As you read, consider the following questions:

1. What is the difference between an Uzi and the semiautomatic rifles banned by Bill Clinton, according to Perkins?
2. How do the banned semiautomatic rifles compare with standard hunting rifles, according to Lott?
3. How do rank and file police officers feel about gun control, as cited by the author?

Reprinted from Joseph Perkins, "Banning Semiautomatics Won't Stop Violence," *San Diego Union-Tribune*, April 17, 1998, with permission.

Hardly any American would dispute that there is far too much gun-related violence in our society. Not when there are more gun deaths in the United States each year than in any other nation in the civilized world.

The politicians would have the crime-fearing public believe that the simple way to reduce gun-related violence is to enact more gun controls. Thus, President Clinton's recent executive order banning importation of nearly six dozen types of so-called "assault weapons."

"As everyone knows, you don't need an Uzi to go deer hunting," the president said, with 15 uniformed law enforcement officers standing behind him in what the White House described as a silent show of support. "You don't need an AK-47 to go skeet shooting. These are military weapons of war."

Now one needn't be a "gun extremist"—the latest put-down assigned to folks who fear erosion of their Second Amendment right to keep and bear arms—to take issue with the president's remarks or to question the efficacy of his executive order.

Indeed, based on the president's sound bite, you would think that, until his executive order last week, the nation's gun sellers were importing Uzis and AK-47s like they were going out of style. But, in fact, these weapons were already banned under a provision of the 1994 crime bill.

The White House claims that the 58 semiautomatic weapons covered under the president's executive order are variations of the Uzi and AK-47. They accuse foreign gun makers of making cosmetic changes to get around the 1994 assault weapons ban.

But the White House is exploiting the public's ignorance of differences between semiautomatic and automatic weapons. The Israeli-made Uzi and Russian-made AK-47 are automatic rifles that fire multiple rounds with each pull of trigger, much like a rapid-fire machine gun.

The semiautomatic "assault weapons" that the president banned fire only one round per trigger pull, which is quite different from the "weapons of war" that the president talked about.

Moreover, notes John Lott Jr., a fellow at the University of Chicago School of Law, the 58 imported "assault weapons" banned by the president are no different than semiautomatic weapons sold here in the United States.

"They are not more powerful," according to Lott, "they don't shoot any faster and they don't shoot any more rounds. Indeed," he continues, "the particular guns that were banned use smaller cartridges—and thus possess less killing power—than standard hunting rifles."

And here's something else the crime-fearing public ought to know about so-called "assault weapons"—they account for fewer than 1 percent of firearms recovered at crime scenes. Indeed, more Americans are bludgeoned to death each year than are murdered by semiautomatic rifles.

But the president doesn't want to hear this—because it undermines the administration's effort to broaden the definition of "assault weapons" as part of its unspoken, incremental effort to ban semiautomatic rifles. The White House also doesn't want to acknowledge that, while many of the nation's police chiefs pay lip service to the administration's gun control agenda, rank and file cops feel differently.

This was borne out by a 1997 survey of 2,000 sworn members of the San Diego Police Department which revealed that 82 percent opposed an assault weapons ban, 94 percent said that recent gun laws (including weapons bans, magazine capacity limits and longer waiting periods) have not reduced violent crime in their service area, and 92 percent said that further restrictive gun laws will not decrease violent crime.

ASSAULT RIFLE CRIMES ARE NEGLIGIBLE

Assault-gun collectors aren't arming to face an invasion of chipmunks. Should we care if a million or two assault rifles are ordered and oiled and occasionally fired on the range? The statistics, as acknowledged by the *Washington Post*, are pretty reassuring: The rifles aren't used, except in statistically negligible cases, for the commission of crime. Where they are used, more modest weapons would have served about as well.

William F. Buckley, *National Review*, May 18, 1998.

The sentiments of these San Diego police officers were perhaps best expressed by Officer Roy Huntington, in a commentary he authored last year. "Cops," he wrote, "are disgusted with being ordered to pose formally behind self-appointed 'community leaders' and governmental bigwigs for publicity photos. This serves to convey the illusion we support the uninformed garbage they are attempting to foist upon an often sadly unsuspecting public."

Indeed, it would be wondrous if the president's latest ban on imported semiautomatic rifles reduced the amount of gun-related violence in this country. But the president knows—and the American people ought to know—that it will have less than zero effect.

7

"Many criminal records are not
'instantaneously' accessible—the
five-day waiting period gives law
enforcement officials the time needed
to complete an adequate background
check."

WAITING PERIODS PREVENT CRIMINALS FROM PURCHASING HANDGUNS

Handgun Control, Inc.

Handgun Control, Inc. (HCI) is a national organization that advocates gun control regulation. In the following viewpoint, HCI
argues that a waiting period with an accompanying background
check is the best way to prevent criminals from illegally purchasing handguns. Many criminal records are not computerized,
the organization maintains, and therefore law enforcement officials need the waiting period in which to complete an adequate
background check. A system that instantly checks a gun purchaser's background without a waiting period frequently re-
turns incomplete records, HCI contends, and would allow many
criminals to buy handguns.

As you read, consider the following questions:

1. What is a beneficial side effect of the five-day waiting period,
   according to HCI?
2. What percentage of criminal records were computerized in
   1995, as cited by Handgun Control?
3. How many prohibited gun purchasers were prevented from
   buying a handgun under the Brady Law, according to the U.S.
   Department of Justice?

Reprinted from "National 'Instant Check' for Handgun Purchases: No Substitute for
Waiting Period and Manual Background Check," by Handgun Control, Inc. (1997), at
www.handguncontrol.org/helping/instantcheck.htm, with permission.

The Brady Handgun Violence Prevention Act (Brady or Brady Law), in its original form, required a five-day waiting period and background check before completion of the sale of a handgun. Although the U.S. Supreme Court ruled on June 27, 1997, that background checks on handgun purchasers are no longer mandatory under federal law, the court left intact the five-day waiting period and the requirement that a "National Instant Criminal Background Check System" replace the waiting period in December 1998. At that time, all background checks would utilize a national, computerized database to screen handgun buyers.

Until the instant check system was implemented, almost every state and local government continued to perform background checks either voluntarily or because they are required by state law. In fact, a national survey of law enforcement found that 94.4% of all police departments continued to do the background checks, despite the Supreme Court's ruling.

DISADVANTAGES OF THE "INSTANT CHECK" SYSTEM

• Implementation of the "instant check" eliminates the benefits of the five-day waiting period. The waiting period serves as a valuable "cooling off" period; too many murders and suicides are completed within hours of a handgun purchase. In addition, many criminal records are not "instantaneously" accessible—the five-day waiting period gives law enforcement officials the time needed to complete an adequate background check.

• The "instant check" system sacrifices accuracy and reliability for the convenience of gun owners. An "instant check" system guarantees that "law-abiding" gun owners can buy a gun within a few minutes, but it does not guarantee that criminals will be stopped from buying guns.

• An "instant check" is not always an "accurate check." A national "instant check" system relies on information that is accessible by federal computers. When local law enforcement officials conduct a background check, they generally consult local, state and federal records, using both computerized and non-computerized data bases.

• The "instant check" system is not ready. By necessity, an "instant check" system relies upon information that is complete and instantly accessible. But many criminal records are not complete, not computerized, or not currently accessible by a national "instant check system." The Justice Department reported that in 1995 only one-third of the 52 million criminal history records in this country have dispositions, are computerized, and are accessible for interstate use by law enforcement.

• States with criminal history records that are adequately computerized can exempt themselves from the Brady Law and the required waiting period by establishing an "instant check" system. Several states, in fact, have already done so. But some states—like Maine and West Virginia—are simply not capable of implementing such a system because their records are not computerized.

COVERING THE COST OF AN INSTANT CHECK SYSTEM

The creation and operation of the Instant Check system is very expensive. The FBI projects that 11.4 million background checks will be conducted annually, with the FBI performing an estimated 4.9 million checks directly and states completing the remainder. The FBI also projects that it will need a staff of more than 500 just to research the cases flagged by Instant Check as "delayed." The Justice Department estimated in August 1998 that the cost of the NICS for fiscal year 1999 would be $91.6 million.

Violence Policy Center, *Paper Tiger? Will the Brady Law Work After Instant Check?*, 1998.

• Don't mess with success. The Brady Law is working. According to the U.S. Department of Justice, since the Brady Law went into effect, background checks nationwide have stopped approximately 250,000 felons and other prohibited purchasers from buying handguns; including 157 felons per day. Termination of the Brady waiting period (and local background checks) could lead to a sharp decrease in the number of denials; many criminals would still be buying handguns at gun stores.
• The Brady Law authorized $200 million for the improvement of state criminal records, and Congress appropriated $125 million in fiscal year 1995 and 1996. Of that amount—$112 million—already has been awarded in direct grants to state and local governments.

"Instead of merely denying the [illegal gun] purchase and letting [the criminal] go—which is all the Brady Act does—Instant Check states can dispatch officers and effect an instant arrest."

INSTANT BACKGROUND CHECKS WOULD PREVENT CRIMINALS FROM PURCHASING HANDGUNS

Tanya K. Metaksa

In the following viewpoint, Tanya K. Metaksa argues that the Brady Act—which requires a background check during a waiting period before a purchaser can take possession of a handgun—has little effect on criminals who purchase handguns. Most criminals do not buy their guns from a gun dealer, she contends, and those that attempt to do so are rarely prosecuted. A better alternative to the waiting period is an instant background check, Metaksa asserts, in which law enforcement officers can be instantly dispatched to arrest those attempting to make an illegal gun purchase. Metaksa is the executive director of the National Rifle Association Institute for Legislative Action.

As you read, consider the following questions:

1. How many illegal purchasers have been detected by the Brady Law since 1994, as cited by the author?
2. Of those illegal purchasers, how many have been imprisoned, according to Metaksa?
3. How many criminals have been imprisoned in Virginia under the Instant Check and Arrest program, according to the author?

Reprinted from Tanya K. Metaksa, "Why the Brady Act Doesn't Work," *The Washington Times*, February 28, 1997, with permission from *The Washington Times*. Copyright ©1997 News World Communications, Inc.

One night you work late and return home, only to find police cars surrounding your house. Your heart pounds as you approach the police officer at your front door. "A stranger tried to break in," he explains, "but your neighbor called 911. We caught the criminal in the act and cuffed him." You breathe a sigh of relief, but the relief soon vanishes. Incredibly, the officer walks the criminal down the street and releases him.

THE SYSTEM NEEDS ANOTHER LOOK

Since 1994, the officer explains, authorities have detected as many as 100,000 criminals in the act of breaking the law—only to free virtually every one of them. In fact, between 1994 and 1997, only three have been imprisoned. "I don't like it either," the officer shrugs, "but it's the system."

If you think that sort of "system" warrants another look, you ought to take another look at the Brady Act. Because purporting to detect 100,000 criminals breaking the law—only to imprison a grand total of three—is exactly what the Clinton administration is getting away with—even boasting about.

The Bureau of Alcohol, Tobacco and Firearms tells us that the vast majority of criminals don't buy guns in stores anyway. They steal them or get them on the black market. With the Brady Act failing to arrest, prosecute and ultimately incarcerate that rare prohibited person who attempts a purchase, it's no wonder academics give the law the cold shoulder.

"It is hard to see the Brady law heralded by many politicians, the media, and Handgun Control, Inc. as an important step toward keeping handguns out of the hands of dangerous and irresponsible persons, as anything more than a sop to the widespread fear of crime," concluded New York University researchers Kimberly Potter and James Jacobs, the latter the Director of the Center for Research in Crime and Justice.

BRADY IGNORES THE LAW

The General Accounting Office (GAO) doesn't give the law passing marks either. After a 15-month review, GAO could find only three felons incarcerated under the law for attempting illegal gun purchases. That's a mighty small number for a mighty big crime. A felon who even attempts to get a gun can be put away for five years. That's federal law. Rather than support that law, the Brady Act essentially ignores it—the very regulation on which all Americans can agree, namely, that criminals who try to get guns belong behind bars.

GAO concluded, "Brady may not result in measurable reductions of gun-related crimes." Clinton's former deputy attorney general, put an even finer point on it; Phillip Heymann wrote in the *Washington Post* "None of [the current reductions in crime] is the result of the president's temporary new cops, nor the Brady Act . . ."

A BETTER WAY

There is a better way. It's even built into the Brady Act. Many of the lawmakers who voted for Brady did so only because it contained a requirement to upgrade criminal records even further, and to evolve into that better way. In 1998, the Brady wait expired, and the National Instant Check and Arrest took its place. Gun ban advocates are sure to push for an extension—even a permanent waiting period—but that just postpones the onset of a system that has proven to be fast, fair and effective in more than a dozen states.

HANDCUFFS, NOT HANDGUNS

In 1993, when the Brady Act went into effect there were 5 states operating the instant check and arrest system. Today, there are 15. The arrests record of the Brady Act pales in comparison to that of the instant check states. Two stellar regional examples are Virginia and Delaware.

Virginia was the first state to implement the instant check and arrest system in 1987. At the time Sarah Brady called it "a model for the nation." Since 1989, the instant check system has led to the arrest of more than 2,700 prohibited persons who attempted to purchase firearms in the Commonwealth.

In Delaware, 67% of the prohibited persons that walk into a gun store and attempt a purchase, walk out with handcuffs on and are on their way to jail.

It does absolutely no good to just deny felons, you must arrest them to truly prevent them from getting guns.

Wayne LaPierre, National Rifle Association Press Conference, February 28, 1998.

In those states, the police know exactly who the prohibited person is—and where he is—when they're alerted that he's attempting an illegal gun purchase. Instead of merely denying the purchase and letting him go—which is all the Brady Act does—Instant Check states can dispatch officers and effect an instant arrest.

Since 1987, when Virginia became the first state to adopt the system, the State Police have arrested 2,479 criminals, including

304 wanted persons. Since then, wherever it's implemented, Instant Check and Arrest works. In Delaware, a resounding 67 percent of those wanted by authorities who attempted a commercial gun purchase were apprehended on the spot. Not denied. Not turned away. Not given five days to criss-cross the U.S.—but apprehended. No wonder the Oregon state police association lobbied in 1996 to replace the state's 15-day waiting period with Instant Check and Arrest.

It's time to stop waiting and start acting. Indeed, the Supreme Court may well declare the Brady Act unconstitutional any time now. In December 1996, the Supreme Court heard oral arguments on whether or not the Brady Act violated the Constitution by commandeering local and state law enforcement officers and ordering them to implement a federal regulatory program.

TIME TO GET STARTED

So it's time to implement the better way. In the Brady Act Congress wrote the Clinton administration a check for $200 million to further upgrade and automate criminal history records and bring that better system on line. All the federal government has to do is follow the leadership of the states. Delaware implemented the system in six months. So did Florida. Virginia, the first with the system, implemented it in 8 months for $500,000. The Virginia State Police make it easy; they even make the software available to other jurisdictions free of charge.

So there's no reason to wait for the better system. And there's absolutely no reason to excuse criminals from prison terms they so richly deserve.

PERIODICAL BIBLIOGRAPHY

The following articles have been selected to supplement the diverse views presented in this chapter. Addresses are provided for periodicals not indexed in the *Readers' Guide to Periodical Literature*, the *Alternative Press Index*, the *Social Sciences Index*, or the *Index to Legal Periodicals and Books*.

Jeff Brazil and Steve Berry	"Outgunned: The Holes in America's Assault Weapon Laws," *Los Angeles Times*, August 24–27, 1997. Available from Reprints, Times Mirror Square, Los Angeles, CA 90054.
Dana Charry and Ellen Charry	"The Crisis of Violence," *Christian Century*, July 15–22, 1998.
Ted Deeds	"Guns, Crime, Troubled Kids, and Predatory Politicians," *Shield*, Fall 1998. Available from 7700 Leesburg Pike, #421, Falls Church, VA 22043.
Fred Guterl	"Gunslinging in America," *Discover*, May 1996.
Philip J. Hilts	"The New Battle over Handguns," *Good Housekeeping*, June 1997.
David Icke	"Take My Gun . . . Please," *Truth Seeker*, vol. 124, no. 2, 1997. Available from 16935 W. Bernardo Dr., #103, San Diego, CA 92127.
David Kopel	"Burglary and the Armed Homestead," *Chronicles*, January 1998. Available from the Rockford Institute, 928 N. Main St., Rockford, IL 61103.
John R. Lott Jr. and David B. Mustard	"Crime, Deterrence, and Right-to-Carry Concealed Handguns," *Journal of Legal Studies*, January 1997.
Grover G. Norquist	"Have Gun, Will Travel," *American Spectator*, November 1998.
Daniel D. Polsby	"From the Hip," *National Review*, March 24, 1997.

CHAPTER 3

How Should Society Treat Juvenile Offenders?

CHAPTER PREFACE

The image of young men standing in formation being yelled at by a drill instructor, dropping to perform pushups on command, and responding to questions with a polite "yes, sir" or "no, ma'am" has struck a chord with Americans who want their criminal justice system to "get tough" on juvenile offenders. By the mid-1990s, thirty states had established military-style "boot camps" as an alternative to prison or probation for juveniles convicted of nonviolent crimes. The boot camps try to instill in the teens self-respect, discipline, a sense of responsibility, and a work ethic, and to motivate them to find jobs and become productive members of society. Most of the boot camps follow similar regimens: reveille seven days a week at 5 A.M.; followed by grueling marches and drills; physical training and hard labor; academic classes and study; and drug, alcohol, and peer counseling programs; with lights out usually at 9 P.M.

Supporters of the boot camps assert that the boot camps produce positive results for juvenile offenders. Although boot camps in different parts of the country emphasize different programs and features, studies show that most participants improve their reading, writing, and math skills by at least one grade level before graduating from camp. Many of the graduates also learn vocational skills which give them an extra boost in finding jobs after completing boot camp. In addition, because boot camp programs are typically two to four months long, they are generally less expensive to run than traditional prisons.

Critics charge, however, that boot camps have a big drawback: they are no more effective at reducing recidivism rates than imprisonment. Study after study has shown that juveniles who participate in boot camp programs commit new crimes and are sent back to prison at rates that are nearly identical to those who were incarcerated. The main problem with boot camps, the opponents maintain, is that the programs are too short. "You can't correct 14 or 15 years in 45 days," contends Larry Meyers, director of juvenile programs for the American Correctional Association. "It's a setup for failure." Opponents concede, however, that boot camps that incorporate counseling and follow-up supervision have lower recidivism rates than prisons and camps that do not offer such programs.

The debate over the effectiveness of boot camps for juvenile offenders reveals how difficult it is to find a one-size-fits-all solution to juvenile crime. The authors in the following chapter examine other measures to combat criminal behavior in the nation's youth.

"When young criminals kill and rape, they should be treated like adults, even executing them!"

VIOLENT JUVENILE CRIMINALS SHOULD BE TREATED AS ADULTS

Part I: Morgan Reynolds, Part II: Don Boys

In Part I of the following two-part viewpoint, Morgan Reynolds argues that the juvenile justice system is incapable of handling today's violent teens. He asserts that instead of maintaining two courts—one for adults and one for juveniles—the two should be combined into a system for all age groups. In Part II, Don Boys contends that juveniles must be held accountable and treated like adults for their crimes. Juvenile crime will continue to be a serious problem until punishment for crimes committed by teens is swift, sure, and severe. Reynolds is the director of the Criminal Justice Center at the National Center for Policy Analysis. Boys is a former Indiana representative and the international director of Common Sense for Today, a conservative Christian think tank.

As you read, consider the following questions:

1. According to Reynolds, what causes crime?
2. What is the most valid predictor of repeat adult crimes, according to studies cited by Boys?
3. What should be the punishment for nonviolent juvenile offenders, in Boys' opinion?

Part I: Reprinted from Morgan Reynolds, "Abolish the Juvenile Justice System?" *Intellectual Ammunition*, November/December 1996, by permission of *Intellectual Ammunition*, a publication of the Heartland Institute, a Chicago-based public policy research organization. Part II: Reprinted from Don Boys, "Criminal Children: The Lunacy of Leniency," at the Common Sense for Today website: www.cst-cc.org/Code/CrimChld.html, by permission of the author.

I

Juvenile crime is a serious problem. The facts are grim: the number of juvenile murderers has tripled to 3,100 since 1984, and 125,000 youths are charged each year with a serious violent crime. One person in five arrested for a violent crime is seventeen years old or less, although kids ages five to seventeen represent only 15.5 percent of the population.

The only good news lately is that the arrest rate for juvenile violent crimes dropped 2.9 percent in 1995. The bad news, however, is that by 2005 the population of males ages fourteen to twenty-four will grow by 1.8 million. Judging from the past, the most vicious 7 percent of those will commit most youthful crimes of violence, implying an expansion of 125,000 criminals over the next nine years.

WHAT CAUSES CRIME?

What causes crime? We don't need a lot of sociological mumbo-jumbo to answer this question. The guilty criminal does! He (93 percent of offenders are male) is a free moral agent who, confronted with a choice between right and wrong, chooses to do wrong, even if only for a brief period in his life. He refuses to respect the rights of others to be secure in their lives and possessions.

The causes of our juvenile crime problem are twofold: 1) more youths than ever are effectively growing up as barbarians, failing to adopt the minimum ethics required for peaceful cooperation, and 2) crime "pays" for too many youths—they usually pay a low price even when caught.

The way to solve America's juvenile crime problem is to rebuild internal restraints, decentralize and pare back the welfare state, increase competition and choice in schools, and strengthen the family and private-sector control generally. It would be nice if "prevention" remedies could do the whole job, but expecting that would be naive. As one Texas judge put it, "A half-grow'd rattlesnake is about as dangerous as a full-grow'd one." The price of crime must be raised.

The primary obstacle to such reform is the juvenile justice system. Virtually everyone except those employed in it recognizes its failure. The system is founded on false premises because it intends to shield youths from the consequences of their own actions.

The first juvenile court was created in Chicago in 1899. The idea quickly spread across the nation, promoted by the same Progressive movement that earlier had pushed such reforms as rehabilitation, probation, parole, and the indeterminate sentence. Individualized treatment by social workers and other experts devoted to the child's "best interest" became the new elixir.

YOUTH IS NOT AN EXCUSE

Besides displacing the guidance of parents, church, and community, such an approach violates the fundamental principles of justice. Youth shouldn't be an excuse. As Judge Ralph Adam Fine of Wisconsin says, "We keep our hands out of a flame because it hurt the very first time (not the second, fifth, or tenth time) we touched fire." Yet the juvenile courts still handle 1.4 million delinquency cases each year, including 100,000 serious violent crimes.

The principles of justice are symbolized by the blindfold, balance scales, and sword of Justitia. One system with equal justice for all—not separate systems for different groups—serves us best. Youth can still serve as a mitigating circumstance in sentencing and separate correctional facilities may continue. But asked whether juveniles convicted of their second or third crimes should be given the same punishment as adults, 83 percent of those surveyed say, "Yes."

Rules operate through the expectations they create. They must be tough, fair and apply to all, free of arbitrariness, privilege, and discrimination. But what do we get from Washington? One year it's midnight basketball, the next it's curfews. All the more reason to rely on a decentralized approach. State and local governments have been toughening their treatment of young criminals. The logical end of these new measures is to abolish the welfare approach to young criminals in favor of justice.

II

Our city streets are dark, dirty, dangerous and are often dominated by raping, robbing and rampaging children. In 1992, juvenile courts handled 2,500 criminal homicides and over a million cases of lesser crimes. We are seeing more and more very young people commit serious, sordid and sadistic crimes—some kids as young as six! As families, homes and churches implode, a subculture of juvenile criminals has developed.

Juveniles used to be considered young, athletic, students with ruddy complexion, squeaky voice and acne, but now they are often vindictive, vicious and violent criminals.

We have been assured that "there is no such thing as a bad boy" (or girl); however, the fact is, there is no such thing as a good boy (or girl). No kid has to be taught to lie, steal, talk back, rebel, etc. It is human nature. Theologians call it the "fallen nature," as a result of original sin. But since that is not politically correct, men have been conned into believing all people are basically good—then we try to justify and explain why "good" people commit outrageously brutal crimes.

THE JUVENILE JUSTICE SYSTEM

Part of the problem of juvenile crime is the criminal justice system itself. While ours may be the "best in the world" (what does that say about the rest of the world?), it is long overdue for a major overhaul. . . .

Kids must no longer have a free ride until age 18. They must get the message that they will be held accountable for their actions with their names and photos published in the media, and their record following them if they continue into adult crime. Studies show that a juvenile's crime record is one of the most valid predictors of repeat adult crime.

Mike Ramirez. Reprinted by permission of Copley News Service.

Young criminals should not be in school, and while the bleeding hearts whine about those kids, I prefer to show my concern for the large group who want to learn. Put the violent kids in a boot camp where they can be made into "young marines" under the tutelage of a traditional leatherneck trained at Parris Island.

Get them up at 5:00 a.m., feed them a big breakfast and work them until they drop. Absolutely no back talk and only magic words such as "yes sir," "no sir," "please," and "thank you, sir" would be permitted. And no psychologist, psychiatrist, social worker or lawyer within 100 miles!

Those kids who are involved in nonviolent crime would be treated less severely. They would be forced to make restitution to their victims, clean up any mess they made and spend time in structured community service.

SWIFT, SURE, AND SEVERE JUSTICE

Kids must learn that justice will be swift, sure and severe in the courts, if not at home and school. Personal accountability will be the reality from now on. That will appall many social scientists and psychologists who tell us that a person is not responsible for personal actions. It all goes back, we are told, to poor potty training, low self-esteem, poor living conditions, etc., so a young person should not be held to an accounting for his crimes. My intellectual reply is poppycock, balderdash and a generous portion of hogwash.

We are told that kids murder, mug and maim because they grew up in poverty; however, poverty doesn't cause crime; crime causes poverty! Juveniles, like adults, commit crimes because they choose to do so. And they must be held accountable.

When young criminals kill and rape, they should be treated like adults, even executing them! Most of us are horrified at that thought but if capital punishment can be defended then who is to say one must be 21? If a 16-year-old commits a vicious murder, who says he should not pay with his life? Of course, there must be an age below which a child would not be executed, but that is a political decision made in each state.

So the message to kids should be clear, concise and conclusive. No free ride until 18. No anonymity. No blaming poverty, parents or potty training for criminality. No more community service for rape and murder. Even the most dull teen will understand that society considers leniency lunacy and a thing of the past.

Kids think they can get away with murder and they will continue to believe that until citizens force the criminal justice system to get its act together. When a few teens "walk the last mile" other teens will get the message that sane, sensible and scared people are taking over from the bleeding hearts.

The radical leftist, upon reading this, will stand up and on cue, bleed all over himself; however, my heart bleeds for the innocent victims.

"Recidivism rates actually are lower for adolescents who are punished in juvenile court as opposed to those who find themselves in the adult criminal system."

JUVENILE CRIMINALS SHOULD NOT BE TREATED AS ADULTS

Jo-Ann Wallace

The following viewpoint is Jo-Ann Wallace's testimony before the House of Representatives' Subcommittee on Crime. Wallace, the director of the public defender service for the District of Columbia, argues that the juvenile court system should not be abolished. Treating juveniles harshly or giving them adult sentences does not reduce the incidence of juvenile crimes, she contends. In fact, Wallace maintains, statistics show that juveniles prosecuted in adult courts have a higher rate of recidivism than juveniles who were tried in juvenile courts. Moreover, children do not have the same rights and responsibilities as adults, nor are they mature enough to understand the consequences of their actions. Therefore, she asserts, children should not be tried in adult courts or sentenced to adult prison time.

As you read, consider the following questions:

1. Why should a juvenile's court records be protected from public scrutiny, according to William Rehnquist?
2. What are some consequences of a policy that would treat juveniles like adults, according to the author?
3. How does prosecuting a juvenile in an adult court encourage crime, in Wallace's opinion?

Reprinted from Jo-Ann Wallace, statement before the Subcommittee on Crime, Committee on the Judiciary, U.S. House of Representatives, Hearing on H.R. 3565 (Violent Youth Predator Act of 1996) and H.R. 3445 (Balanced Juvenile Justice and Crime Prevention Act of 1996), June 27, 1996.

We all want crime reduced, crime generally, and juvenile and violent crime specifically. The question is: Does treating children like adults work?

The best evidence that we have so far is that the answer is no. The empirical evidence tells us that a juvenile justice system built on harsh penalties does not deter crime. In the District of Columbia, where I practice, we have the highest per capita rate of children in custody of anywhere in the country. Yet, there's a serious juvenile crime problem.

No Evidence

In the District of Columbia, children 16 and over are prosecuted like adults and they face life imprisonment like adults, but there is no evidence—the statistics do not bear out that 16-year-olds facing life sentences in adult facilities are committing fewer violent crimes than 15-year-olds facing prosecution as juveniles. In fact, the statistics and the other evidence is to the contrary. Studies show that recidivism rates actually are lower for adolescents who are punished in juvenile court as opposed to those who find themselves in the adult criminal system.

[It has been] suggested that adolescents who are treated in juvenile court somehow get off lightly. Well, in fact, not only do the studies show that the juvenile court system is more effective at deterring future crime, but the studies also show that an individual, a youth, is more likely to spend more time in the juvenile system for an offense—for example, drug offenses—than they would if they were put into the adult system. Moreover, there is no evidence at all which shows that mandatory minimum sentences, which studies reveal are not effective in reducing adult recidivism, will be any more effective in deterring juvenile crime.

Why Stiff Penalties Do Not Work

There are a lot of reasons why stiff penalties don't work for juveniles, but the first and foremost reason is because children and adolescents are impulsive. They usually do not do a cost-benefit analysis before they engage in antisocial behavior. This has been recognized since time immemorial. Those of you, if any, who have survived raising an adolescent know this to be true. I haven't been there yet. In fact, I have many child-rearing years ahead of me before I can wear that badge of honor, but my colleagues who have survived that trauma assure me that what I have to look forward to with each child is at least one major lapse in judgment.

The undisputed fact of life that adolescents think and act differently than adults is a bedrock principle around which much of our society revolves. Apart from being the solid premise upon which our juvenile justice system is built, it is the reason why the law recognizes a host of distinctions between the rights and duties of children and those of adults. Because they may not foresee the consequences of their decisions, a minor may not, for example, enforce a bargain, may not lawfully work or travel where he pleases, or even attend exhibitions of constitutionally-protected adult movies. Persons below a certain age may not vote, may not buy certain items like cigarettes or alcohol, and may not marry without parental consent.

So it seems incongruous to me that, because of the inherent disabilities of his or her age, no 14-year-old may qualify to serve on a jury; yet, a 14-year-old may be tried by a jury and sentenced to life in prison. Nothing that we know about young people growing up today suggests that the differences that have been true forever of adolescence is any less true now.

PROTECTING THE JUVENILE COURT RECORDS

The protection which juvenile court affords the child extends to his or her court records because, as then-Justice William Rehnquist said, "It's important for the rehabilitative goal. The widespread dissemination of a juvenile offender's name may defeat the beneficent and rehabilitative purposes of a State's juvenile justice system."

Justice Rehnquist in that case cited a study which concluded that publicity really does have a negative impact, and that—in fact, it did have a negative impact on that particular young person—that it interfered with his adjustment at various points when he was otherwise proceeding adequately. Other studies confirm that publicity detracts from rehabilitation. For some juvenile offenders publicity provides a sense of importance that actually encourages, rather than discourages, delinquent behavior. And for others the stigma of the public label becomes a self-fulfilling prophecy because, once a youth is rejected by many in society, his only recourse is to adopt friends who encourage his antisocial behavior. In addition—and this cannot be overemphasized—publicity makes it even more difficult to find a job, a crucial factor in a juvenile's ability to avoid slipping further into delinquency.

THE CONSEQUENCES OF SENDING JUVENILES TO PRISON

While there is no evidence that treating more juveniles like adults will reduce crime, there is plenty of evidence of other consequences of such policy. Studies show that more children will be beaten, sexually molested, kill themselves, and be killed at the hands of adults. Seventeen-year-old Damico Watkins is one recent example. While he was serving a 7- to 25-year sentence for acting as a lookout in a pizza shop robbery, he was stabbed to death by seven adults in an Ohio prison.

When the justice system becomes a party that enables children to be killed at the hands of adults, the price is at least twofold. First, there is a loss of public confidence in a system whose primary function is supposed to be to protect its citizens, and then there is the very tangible cost in dollars resulting from mounting civil actions, as aggrieved families and communities attempt to have their wrongs redressed.

CHILDREN ARE NOT JUST SHORT ADULTS

The juvenile justice system is not based upon some unfinished or outdated liberal agenda. It is based upon the social fact that children are not fully developed moral beings and cannot, in our system of jurisprudence, be held as accountable as adults for their wrongdoing. A child does not have the same degree of empathetic capacity, cognitive skills, judgment, and impulse control as does a mature adult. Children don't formulate intent, in the same manner as adults, and American justice punishes according to the intent not simply the act. There is a difference between a 14-year-old robber and a 25-year-old robber.

The juvenile system is based on the well understood and scientifically established fact that children get into trouble because bad things have happened to them. Nearly all of our violent offenders are abused, traumatized, neglected, or mentally ill children who come from violent surroundings and dysfunctional families. Most are in the midst of grinding poverty, adolescent identity development, and tremendous peer pressure. Many live day-to-day, moment-to-moment, drama-to-drama. Is it really a surprise that these seriously troubled kids are getting into serious trouble? Consequence and deterrence, by the way, are essentially meaningless concepts when applied to children who don't know they have a future, or worse, know they have none.

Stephen K. Harper, *Juvenile Justice Update*, August/September 1998.

The decision to prosecute an adolescent as an adult more often encourages, rather than discourages, future crime. Once a youth is transferred to adult court, he or she is subject to the same harsh penalties. The adult facilities in which they are housed, as you've heard, are not only dangerous, they generally provide no rehabilitative services.

Unfortunately, I have seen far too much confirmation of the statistics which show that secure facilities that warehouse children do not prevent crime. I personally have watched naive youngsters grow into hardened, streetwise adolescents behind a razor-wire fence. Such institutions reinforce self-images as outlaws. They produce youth who fall so far behind in school that they know they can't catch up, and they don't even try.

Moreover, the children who will suffer the harmful consequences of adult treatment will be—there's no real question about it—disproportionately minority youth. Statistics and studies undeniably demonstrate that minority youth are overrepresented in the juvenile justice system. This is true in every stage of the system—from arrest to disposition and sentencing—and this is true in all parts of the country. It is also the case that more minority youth are more likely to be transferred to adult court than their white counterparts. Of course, when mandatory minimums are added to the mix, the racial disparities become even more pronounced.

NOT AN EFFECTIVE POLICY

The automatic treatment of juveniles like adults for certain categories of offenses is neither an effective crime policy nor a cost-effective fiscal policy. Statistics show that, contrary to popular belief, really more than half—in fact, somewhere around 60 percent at least—of youth who enter the juvenile justice system do not return. Particularly when mandatory minimums come into play, you can calculate that such policies result in huge amounts of wasted monetary resources, given the $35,000 to $60,000 per year that it costs to incarcerate an individual youth.

I'll end where I started. I believe that the citizens of this nation are looking for results. We are looking for cost-effective, crime-reduction policies that work. Treating children more like adults is not tough on crime; it is simply ineffectively tough on kids.

"It is hardly arbitrary or
unreasonable for a community to
regulate an activity—even when the
activity is engaged in by entirely
innocent people—when that activity
frequently leads to harmful
consequences for others."

SOCIETY SHOULD IMPOSE CIVIL ORDINANCES AGAINST GANGS

Roger Conner

In 1992, Chicago enacted an anti-gang ordinance that prohibited gang members from loitering with other gang members in certain locations. In the following viewpoint, Roger Conner argues that these gang injunctions should be upheld by the courts. Government should be able to regulate activities that harm the community, he contends, even if the ordinances infringe upon the rights of innocent people. Restricting gang loitering helps reduce gang violence and makes the surrounding community safer, Conner maintains. Conner is executive director of the Center for the Community Interest, an advocacy group for public safety and urban quality-of-life issues.

As you read, consider the following questions:

1. What three requirements must be fulfilled before a Chicago police officer can order loitering gang members to disperse, according to Conner?
2. What is the author's response to charges that ordinances and civil injunctions used against gangs are racist?

Reprinted from Roger Conner, "Rights for Gangs, Handcuffs for Neighborhoods," *The Responsive Community*, Fall 1998, by permission.

May communities regulate loitering, or is the term so inherently vague as to be unconstitutional? Should police be allowed to order members of criminal gangs and their friends to move on rather than loiter in a group at known gang locations? These are the questions raised in *Chicago v. Morales*, a case before the US Supreme Court in 1998.

Chicago is a city beset by gangs. Well-organized groups engage in drug selling, gun running, robbery, and violence. They control entire neighborhoods by loitering in key locations as a group, by engaging in numerous "low-level" crimes (i.e., graffiti, vandalism, verbal intimidation, urinating openly, etc.), and by occasional use of violent force against perceived rivals or opponents. While only a handful of the gang members actually beat, maim, rob, or kill, the rest enjoy the deference that derives from the violent acts of their colleagues by openly announcing their affiliation through distinctive colors and "uniforms." Ordinary citizens assume, with good reason, that affronts to any member of the group will trigger retaliation. Thus the loitering itself is a way by which a gang announces that it controls a territory, that neither the police nor the community can touch them.

Gangs and the people in their neighborhoods understand the significance of loitering by groups of people. But what can be done? Other than loitering with others, the gang members do not engage in illegal conduct when the police are present. And placing undercover officers nearby would be useless, since most of the gang members never engage in anything other than the lower level offenses that would never produce much in the way of jail time. Is there no remedy?

THE PEOPLE VERSUS THE COURT

After hearings attended by hundreds of residents (one group brought 10,000 signatures), the city council, in May of 1992, approved the following ordinance:

> Whenever a police officer observes a person he reasonably believes to be a criminal gang member loitering in any public place with one or more other persons, he shall order all such persons to disperse and remove themselves from the area. Any person who does not promptly obey such an order is in violation of this section.

By its terms, the ordinance forbade loitering by any group that included "criminal gang members." Before any enforcement could begin, it required the police department to issue general orders—tantamount to administrative rules. The general orders limit and control the discretion of individual officers in several ways. The ordinance may be invoked only at locations that have been specifically designated by a district commander, in consultation with community groups. "Only areas frequented by members of criminal street gangs which, because of their location, significantly affect the activities of law-abiding persons in the surrounding community shall be designated," according to the rule. The officer must have probable cause to believe that a member of the loitering group is a "criminal gang" member, defined as identifiable groups whose members have been convicted of serious offenses (such as murder, armed robbery, aggravated battery on a child or senior citizen, etc.). Only officers from the gang unit or who have received specific training in identification of gang members may make arrests.

In November 1996, the Illinois Supreme Court ruled that the ordinance is unconstitutional, giving two reasons. First, they wrote, the prohibition on loitering is so vague that police are given too much discretion to decide whom to stop and citizens cannot tell how to comply with the law. Second, the ordinance violates due process because it intrudes "arbitrarily or in an utterly unreasonable manner" on the "right" to loiter. Of course, the Constitution does not mention loitering alongside freedom of speech and the right to a jury trial. However, citing Supreme Court cases from the civil rights era, the court held that the right to loiter is embedded in the Constitution. "Persons suspected of being in criminal street gangs are deprived of the personal liberty of being able to freely walk the streets and associate with friends, regardless of whether they are actually gang members or have committed any crime," the court stated.

A Strange Jurisprudence: Ignoring the Actual Ordinance

Let us look at the court's concerns one at a time. First is the issue of "vagueness," of giving the police too much discretion. Of course, a major thrust of community policing is to give police more discretion to address certain types of actions. The "broken windows" theory says that police should address disorder and low-level offenses in order to prevent more serious crimes. This case is a classic example. The city says that if the loitering groups are permitted to remain they will attract violent attacks by other gang members; they will engage in actual violence against people who oppose them; and they will find it easier to conceal activities like drug dealing and robbery upon which their livelihood depends. Loitering by groups that include recognizable gang members is a quintessential "broken window."

To address the problem of *excessive* police discretion, the ordinance includes a requirement that police issue regulations. The regulations that were issued define the factors that an officer should use to decide who is a criminal gang member, and also limit enforcement to specific areas that are designated by a district commander in consultation with community leaders. But the Illinois court refused to even consider whether the regulations were precise enough to limit officer discretion. The Supreme Court needs to stop the lower courts from using the vagueness doctrine to hold such ordinances unconstitutional on their face. In order to throw the ordinance out, the Illinois court should have been forced to find either that the regulations were not precise enough or that the limits were being ignored in practice.

Another "vagueness" concern the court raised concerns not the police, but citizens. How is a person to know if he is in the presence of a gang member? First, as noted, in Chicago gang members thrive on being noticed. They have insignia and colors that are recognized and well-understood by everyone. Still, to remove any doubt, the regulations stipulate that no person has to move along or disperse unless ordered to do so by a police officer. Only then, if the person refuses to move along, does a violation occur.

THE RIGHT TO LOITER

What of the court's second claim, that the ordinance intrudes "arbitrarily or in an utterly unreasonable manner" on the "right" to loiter? Won't enforcement of the ordinance mean that, in some instances, persons who are entirely innocent will be forced to move along? Doesn't this violate their rights to stand around without doing anything wrong? Obviously, some entirely innocent people are going to be forced to move along under this law, and they will resent it. The fact that an eye-popping 45,000 arrests were made in three years suggests how widely the police orders were resisted by gang members and others. Most people feel that they have a right to stand on the sidewalk or park green for no reason, just as we have a right to drive down the street for no reason.

The question is not whether we have a right to loiter any more than the question over traffic sobriety checkpoints is whether we have the right to drive down the street. The real questions are twofold: First, should the community have the power to regulate this activity? Second, is this particular regulation unreasonable?

As to the first, local governments should be permitted to regulate loitering that harms community life. It is one thing for courts to recognize a right to stand or stroll for no reason in public. The error in the Illinois Supreme Court opinion is that it treats loitering as if it were free speech, something that can be regulated in only the most extreme cases.

A Prescription Against Disease

Street gang violence occurs when gang members hang out together, indulge in drugs (both legal and illegal), protect their "claimed" turf and/or molest others over that turf in some manner. Stated oversimplistically, gang violence has been handled by the criminal justice system as a response to the disease affecting a community's wellness.

The use of a restraining order is a prescription against that disease. A restraining order prevents violent gang members from participating in the normal cycle of activities that lead to gang violence. These activities alone may be legal, but when done by documented gang members, they have shown throughout our state to produce only senseless violence and destruction.

Mike Poehlman, North (San Diego) County Times, December 14, 1997.

As to the second question—is this regulation arbitrary or unreasonable—consider this analogy. In most communities it is illegal to drink alcohol from an open container in a public place. Yet most of the people who drink in public places are entirely innocent of any other wrongdoing. Does that fact render the regulation arbitrary or unreasonable? Should such an ordinance be ruled unconstitutional? Few think so. It is hardly arbitrary or unreasonable for a community to regulate an activity—even when the activity is engaged in by entirely innocent people—when that activity frequently leads to harmful consequences for others.

Racism?

A final concern, one not raised by the Illinois court but frequently mentioned by critics of the law, is that this ordinance will be used in a discriminatory fashion. As critics have noted, loitering laws in the '50s and '60s were used in the South to suppress black Americans, and thus they were properly struck down. Today, however, the issue is how to protect the safety of people in minority communities from predatory groups of the same race. Yes, it is true that there is a danger that police will use this ordinance to target groups of blacks or Hispanics rather than using the guidelines to limit its application to persons who police reasonably believe are active gang members. But the same is true of virtually all laws.

The proper way to protect against discrimination is not to rule unconstitutional all statutes that could be misused, but rather to put the plaintiffs to their proofs. In other words, if the ordinance is being misused and plaintiffs can prove it, courts should rule the laws unconstitutional as applied. They should not simply find all such statutes unconstitutional on their face.

A community cannot thrive when its residents are in constant fear for their persons and their property. Acknowledging this reality, the city of Chicago determined, through the democratic process, that the police need to be able to compel groups that include self-announced gang members to disperse. Not allowing the police to do this means the gangs will win and the communities will lose. With this weapon, at least the police and the community will have a chance. The battle to reclaim these communities is already difficult enough. We cannot allow faulty jurisprudence to stand in the way.

"Youth can now be arrested, not
because they do anything illegal, but
because the police think they might
commit a crime!"

IMPOSING CIVIL ORDINANCES AGAINST GANGS IS UNCONSTITUTIONAL

Revolutionary Worker

More and more cities across the United States are using public
nuisance laws in the form of civil injunctions as a weapon in the
war against gangs. The injunctions prohibit gang members from
meeting in public, wearing certain clothing, carrying beepers,
and engaging in other legal behavior. In the following viewpoint, the *Revolutionary Worker* argues that this use of civil injunctions is an infringement of the gang members' civil rights. The
injunctions allow the police to legally harass minorities and
treat them as if they had no rights at all, the *Revolutionary Worker*
maintains. Civil injunctions criminalize a class of people not for
what they have done, the author contends, but for what some
members may do. The *Revolutionary Worker* is a publication of the
Revolutionary Communist Party.

As you read, consider the following questions:

1. What is the justification for using civil injunctions to
   suppress individual rights, in the California Supreme Court's
   opinion, as cited by the author?
2. According to Joan Gallo, what other groups can be included
   under the label of "public nuisance" and subject to civil
   injunctions, as cited by *Revolutionary Worker*?
3. What are some legitimate reasons for teens to be carrying
   pagers and cell phones, according to the author?

Reprinted from "California Supreme Court Ruling: Criminalizing the Youth," editorial,
Revolutionary Worker, February 9, 1997, by permission of RCP Publications, Chicago. (This
article has been retitled and some subheadings were added by Greenhaven editors.)

On January 30, 1997, the California Supreme Court ruled that cities can use "public nuisance laws" to obtain injunctions that prohibit "suspected gang members" from engaging in *legal* activities such as associating on street corners or "annoying" residents.

The 4—3 ruling, overturning a Court of Appeals decision, upheld a 1993 San Jose injunction that prohibited alleged Latino gang members from "standing, sitting, walking, driving, gathering or appearing anywhere in public view" with each other in a four-block neighborhood. The San Jose injunction also barred 38 named individuals from carrying pens, nails or razor blades, from climbing trees or fences and from wearing gang colors in the neighborhood. Each alleged member was served with the injunction and those who violated it faced fines and jail time.

The American Civil Liberties Union challenged the injunction on behalf of 11 of the alleged gang members and the state Court of Appeal in San Jose struck down all parts that prohibited legal activities. The city of San Jose then decided to appeal the parts of the ruling that prevented alleged gang members from associating with, annoying, harassing or threatening residents.

DANGEROUS IMPLICATIONS

The Supreme Court ruling upholding the San Jose injunction has broad and dangerous implications. Nearly a dozen California communities have won similar injunctions and more cities are now expected to seek similar injunctions. L.A. District Attorney Gil Garcetti has announced that he may now seek even broader injunctions to restrict gangs.

The California Supreme Court said that any "rights" people might have under the Constitution are not unconditionally guaranteed to everyone. They said "the freedom of individuals" is less important than the "security of the community." The Court would like people to think their ruling is meant to protect the community. But in reality it is a blatant justification for treating certain sections of the people like they have no rights at all! Amitai Schwartz, a lawyer for the ACLU, which fought against the California ruling said, "These injunctions will sprout up all over the state. And it's not just a matter of gangs. It's a creeping diminution of civil rights, making the courts an arm of the police departments. They relaxed the standards so much that it will undoubtedly be used in other contexts, including labor."

Injunctions like the one in San Jose are made under the authority of "public nuisance laws." Beginning in L.A. in 1987, authorities have used these laws to get injunctions against alleged gang members to prohibit them from doing a long list of legal activities. Under such an injunction the police can arrest people for violating an injunction, and send them to jail for "contempt of court," even if they have committed no other crime. The police also use these injunctions as a legal justification for harassing people.

Every one of these injunctions in California has been issued in a Black or Latino neighborhood. In some places, police have been given the power to arrest youth for all kinds of legal activities—like possessing screwdrivers, cellular phones, two-way radios, beepers, hammers, flashlights, glass bottles, bricks, magic markers, spraypaint, "scribes" for etching, or for using pay phones.

Can you imagine what would happen if the police started arresting doctors, lawyers and other suburban professionals with beepers or cell phones—or middle class homeowners returning from a trip to the hardware store, touching up the paint on their car, or trying to read a map with a flashlight?

The State Supreme Court ruling actually went beyond the San Jose injunction. The court indicated that San Jose would not have been limited to naming specific gang members in the injunction request but could have just named the gang itself to qualify for injunctive relief. This means that cities could name a certain gang in an injunction and on this basis, anyone who the cops think is in the gang could be harassed and arrested.

And there is now talk about using injunctions more broadly. San Jose City Attorney Joan Gallo said the city will now be able to use injunctions to go after other "public nuisances" involving "drugs, liquor stores, bars, nightclubs and apartment complexes."

Stanley Mosk, a State Supreme Court Justice, voted against the decision on the San Jose injunction because he said it would "permit our cities to close off entire neighborhoods to Latino youths who have done nothing more than dress in blue or black clothing or associate with others who do so."

CONSTANT HARASSMENT

The California Supreme Court tried to justify their ruling with talk about "the interests of the community," and "a community's rights to security and protection." And the police try to say people in the community support such injunctions. But the power structure has been behind these police-state type injunctions from the very beginning. In L.A. County, the District Attorney's office has special deputy DAs who go to areas targeted for injunctions, to look for people who want to make complaints about the youth who hang out on the street. The cops get local snitches and backward people to accuse specific youth of all kinds of crimes. The cops don't have to provide any evidence for these charges. The snitches' statements are then sealed by the court. There's no possibility of people defending themselves against false accusations. They don't even know what the accusations are!

OUTLAW COURTS THREATEN SOCIETY

Anger, fear, and frustration over the impotence of law enforcement at curbing illegal gang activity has finally given way to the temptation of the indiscriminate iron-fisted approach embraced by this injunction.

Courts, however, must rise above the common temptation to resort to the shotgun approach to solving such problems. Injunctions must be carefully and narrowly drawn to provide the relief shown to be needed without going further than is absolutely necessary. The court has failed in that obligation in issuing this injunction. Outlaw gangsters threaten the peace and safety of the community but outlaw courts undermine the very foundation of our society.

Gary R. Nichols, *North (San Diego) County Times*, December 14, 1997.

Based on these accusations, a civil court issues a special order that lists all kinds of ordinary things these youth are now forbidden to do. These court orders are handed out to the youth who are named. From then on, the cops can stop and search those youth for doing things that are legal for other people.

Basically, these court orders allow the cops to conduct a constant campaign of harassment against the youth who fit a certain "profile"—it becomes legal for the cops to harass them for simply hanging out, and this makes it hard for these kids to even leave their homes. These youth are treated like they have no rights at all!

INJUNCTION IN INGLEWOOD

The day before the Supreme Court decision, an injunction was issued in Inglewood, a city of 100,000 located next to the L.A. Airport. The injunction prohibits 41 Black youth from using pagers, cell phones or walkie-talkies. The named youth are also barred from gambling and drinking in public and "loitering," that is, standing on the street. The injunction applies to the Black and Latino area of Darby-Dixon. A dozen of the young men targeted by the injunction went to the court hearing and testified that they were not gang members or criminals. But the judge ignored what they had to say and issued the injunction.

Morningside High—"The Side"—is one of two high schools in Inglewood, right on the edge of Darby-Dixon. La Chon, who was hanging out after class, told the *Revolutionary Worker* that she wanted to speak to people in other neighborhoods who "don't have to worry about what we are worrying about." She said, "I go to Morningside High. I struggle every day. I got a 3.8 grade point average. I get good grades. I'm not going around jacking nobody. I'm not going around doing nothing. I'm doing the everyday life, struggling like everybody else. I got a job I attend to every day after school. I live in this area and I work hard just like everybody else on trying to make myself better. But yet they're particularly putting everybody in this area down and I don't think it's right." She said the neighborhood is already full of cops and undercover, and a lot of people get arrested.

A number of other youth from Morningside spoke bitterly about the ban on pagers and cell phones. The capitalists are always talking about the growth of electronic means of communication, calling it the "Information Age." Now the authorities are saying that the oppressed don't have the right to communicate with each other. La Chon noted, "A lot of people got kids, they need their pagers for emergencies and other things like that."

The California Supreme Court has now given cities sweeping powers to step up the power structure's campaign to criminalize youth in Black and Latino neighborhoods. Los Angeles DA Gil Garcetti said, "We are just thrilled that they [the court] have given us one of the most useful tools I have seen as a public prosecutor in 28 years. We don't have to wait for someone to commit a crime to return a community back to law-abiding citizens. This is a process that enables us to go into court to stop criminal activity before it happens." In other words: Black and Latino youth can now be arrested, not because they do anything illegal, but because the police think they might commit a crime!

"It's hard to keep youngsters off the streets during the early morning hours when gangs are roaming if parents don't cooperate."

PARENTS SHOULD BE HELD RESPONSIBLE FOR THEIR CHILDREN'S CRIMES

John Leo

Many states have passed laws which hold parents legally responsible for crimes committed by their children. In the following viewpoint, syndicated columnist John Leo maintains that while parental responsibility laws may have uneven results, they are basically a good idea. Parental responsibility laws may be all that is needed to prod some parents into controlling their children, he contends. However, Leo maintains that because some parents may be unfairly punished for their children's criminal behavior, the laws should be considered experimental and the penalties adjusted accordingly.

As you read, consider the following questions:

1. What are some of the penalties imposed on parents who are convicted of violating parental responsibility laws, as cited by Leo?
2. How are parental responsibility laws sometimes punitive, according to the author?
3. In Leo's opinion, why is the Oregon state measure a better law than the local Silverton ordinance?

Reprinted from John Leo, Commentary, "Parents Must Account for Child's Crimes," U.S. News & World Report, June 14, 1995, with permission. Copyright, 1995, U.S. News & World Report. Visit www.usnews.com for additional information.

In a burst of mostly patronizing publicity from the national media, the small town of Silverton, Oregon, and the Oregon state legislature have moved to hold parents responsible for offenses committed by their children.

"Both stigmatize parents with their assumption that a child's misbehavior results from a failure of parental supervision," clucked a Page One *New York Times* report. And the reporter for public TV's *MacNeil/Lehrer Newshour* explained that Silverton's belief that parents are responsible for children up to age 18 is "a homespun philosophy from a homespun town." (Translation: We are dealing here with a town full of rubes.)

A FAST-GROWING TREND

What the reporter seemed to think was some sort of rural aberration is actually part of a fast-growing national trend. Hundreds of exasperated communities, large and small, are holding parents responsible for curfew violations, graffiti damage and crimes by their children. Often they impose fines or community service, and sometimes require attendance at basic classes on how to parent.

Many changes in welfare plans also make parents responsible for their children's attendance record at school, and in some public housing, a parent can be evicted if a child is found to be dealing drugs out of the family apartment.

In some cases, these laws are popping up in basically stable but apprehensive communities. By big-city standards, the level of vandalism and youth crime in Silverton seems quite low. And in the dozens of Chicago-area communities that now have parental responsibility laws, the targets seem to be illegal teen drinking parties and drunk driving. In these cases, the tactic is chiefly to embarrass well-off parents into taking charge.

"CALL IT QUITS"

In devastated urban areas, however, the practical and ethical problems are very different. It can look as though poor mothers are being punished for the sins of children they can't control. Patricia Holdaway, the first parent charged under the curfew law of Roanoke, Virginia, said: "I went through so much with these kids. I'm just ready to call it quits." Her 16-year-old son, arrested at 5 a.m. for his fifth curfew violation and for driving without a license, said "I just left. It's not her fault. She shouldn't be held responsible. I know right from wrong."

Roanoke's policy is a reasonable one—it wants to work with at-risk youngsters and keep things out of court, if possible. It wants to establish the principle that a mother is responsible to supervise a youngster in trouble. But in this case, the policy led to a $100 fine and a 10-day jail sentence for a woman who already agreed with the principle of parental responsibility but couldn't enforce it. She is appealing the conviction.

A REASONABLE OR DESPERATE ATTEMPT TO CONTROL CHILDREN?

Very few parental responsibility laws allow jail terms. But given the stresses on the poor, many of them single mothers, even mandatory community service or $100 fines can be very punitive. That's why parental responsibility laws catch so many of us leaning both ways, pro and con. Are these laws attempts to reassert reasonable civic expectations about basic parenting, or are they desperate attempts to use the coercive force of the state to solve a cultural problem?

"When a culture is in free fall, as ours is, and our non-legal institutions are falling apart, there's a temptation to move in with laws and government," said David Blankenhorn, president of the Institute for American Values. And the laws work best with parents who are already in control and merely need a wake-up call; they work poorly, or not at all, when the no-parenting ethic is deeply ingrained or passed on from one generation to the next.

TURNING KIDS AROUND

Silverton, Oregon, Police Chief Randy Lunsford maintains the sole purpose of his town's [parental responsibility] ordinance is to help parents do their jobs better. "We're trying to nip it in the bud. We want to make sure the kid who shoplifts today doesn't commit burglary tomorrow. If we can get the parents involved right away, maybe the kid can be turned around."

Carol Sternhell, *Good Housekeeping*, March 1996.

Still many communities are so besieged that something must be tried. It's hard to keep youngsters off the streets during the early morning hours when gangs are roaming if parents don't cooperate. And the detachment of many parents from the fate of their young is a crucial problem—many don't even bother to go down to a police station to collect an arrested son or daughter.

"These laws are signs that the antibodies are starting to kick in," said Roger Connor, head of the American Alliance for Rights and Responsibilities. "But they have to be regarded as experiments. We have to find out what works, what encourages responsibility without resorting to draconian penalties."

Connor thinks the Silverton ordinance is too strong—it allows a fine for offense, requires parental responsibility to age 18, and has been applied to cover teens caught smoking.

THE OREGON MEASURE

The statewide Oregon measure, which has passed the legislature and [was] signed into law by the governor, is more carefully constructed. The law covers responsibility for children up to age 15—a way of recognizing that older teens are much harder to deal with and sometimes beyond parental control. The first offense draws only a warning; the second can require attendance at a parenting class. Only after a third offense can a fine be imposed, and not if the parent can show reasonable efforts to control the child. The offense is civil, not criminal, and the parents cannot be jailed.

With feedback from the community, these laws can be adjusted depending on results and a changing social consensus. Let the experiments continue.

| "If courts use [parental responsibility laws] merely to punish the parents as well as the child, society will gain very little advantage."

PARENTAL RESPONSIBILITY LAWS WILL NOT REFORM DELINQUENT BEHAVIOR

Mary Ann Perga

In the following viewpoint, Mary Ann Perga argues that parental responsibility legislation—laws that hold parents responsible for the crimes of their children—is unlikely to change the behavior of delinquent teens. Many parents will resent the state's interference in their family's daily life, she contends. Furthermore, she asserts that requiring closer supervision of children does not necessarily mean that the children are receiving good parenting and loving attention. The best way to ensure that children grow into responsible adults is to provide volunteer mentors to young children who are at risk of growing up delinquent, she maintains. Perga is a lawyer and columnist for the *Superior Catholic Herald*.

As you read, consider the following questions:

1. When would parental responsibility laws benefit society, in Perga's opinion?
2. What are three problems with parental responsibility laws, according to the author?
3. How does the Big Brother/Big Sister program change children's lives, in Perga's view?

Reprinted from Mary Ann Perga, "Parents Shouldn't Do the Time When Kids Do the Crime," *U.S. Catholic*, December 1996, by permission of *U.S. Catholic*, Claretian Publications, 205 W. Monroe St., Chicago, IL 60606; 800-328-6515.

A short-lived television series called "Dinosaurs" used a society composed entirely of prehistoric creatures to satirize our present society. In one of the episodes, the father, Earl Sinclair, failed a required test and lost his license to parent. A police officer followed him home, and when Earl attempted to discipline his son, the officer told Earl to desist. The officer announced that he was assigned to the home for the next 30 days to ensure that no unauthorized parenting took place. Earl, unable to do anything else, unwillingly complied with the order.

A LICENSE TO PARENT

I do not have children of my own. I learned of my inability to bear children more than 15 years ago. Since that time, I have become a keen observer of the ways people raise their children. Because I am a lawyer who represents those accused of delinquency, I have seen many young lives that have gone astray. A delinquent is a child who commits an act that, if committed by an adult, would be a crime. It is the worst time to meet children. It often saddens me to learn of the many ways in which children's parents have failed them. I have learned enough to know that, in many of these cases, lack of responsible parenting is a contributing cause of the illegal behavior. This observation has sometimes led me to suggest cynically that there should be a license to parent.

Less cynically, I have wished that something practical could be done to deal with irresponsible parents when they were an underlying cause of juvenile delinquency. In many cases it seemed unfair to direct sanctions only against the children. Nothing could be done to the parents in these cases, however, because they were not on trial. That situation has begun to change.

Throughout the country, laws are now being passed that hold parents responsible for the criminal actions of their child if the parents have failed to exercise reasonable parental control. One such law, proposed by a city in Minnesota, would require parents, among other things, to keep illegal drugs and firearms out of their homes, to ensure their children attend school and obey local curfews, to provide or arrange for adequate supervision of their children, and to forbid their children from destroying property or retaining stolen property.

It is easy to understand the motivation for such laws. Juvenile crime is undeniably escalating at record rates throughout the country. The rise in the number of such crimes has been accompanied by an equally disturbing rise in the level of violence. People are frustrated by this situation and are demanding that some action be taken to correct it. Such proposed laws and others like them are passed with the hope that parents will begin to supervise their children more closely. It is believed that prosecutions against some parents who fail in their duties will send a message to other parents. Legislators hope that such laws will ultimately bring about more responsible parenting and, accordingly, be of benefit to children and ultimately to society.

The problem is that the mere passage of a law is not the end of a societal effort, but only the beginning. The way in which the law is applied is crucial to its success. In the hands of concerned judges, these laws may be effective in redirecting the efforts of parents of a troubled child. The most useful time for awakening the parents to the need for change in the home is on the first occasion that the child breaks the law. If the courts begin to require the cooperation of the parents in programs designed to assist them in learning the skills of parenting, the passage of parental responsibility laws will be a useful tool to society.

PROBLEMS WITH PARENTAL RESPONSIBILITY LAWS

The current climate in the country may work against such use of these laws. Many states, including my own state of Wisconsin, have passed legislation that redirects the focus of juvenile courts away from understanding and rehabilitation and toward punishment and retribution. I am concerned that this same direction will be applied to parents found guilty under the responsibility laws. If courts use this legislation merely to punish the parents as well as the child, society will gain very little advantage.

A second problem with this legislation is that it will often come into play far too late to be effective. Few parents look at their younger than 5-year-old child and see a future criminal. Yet this is the very time in the child's life when responsible and loving parenting is essential. Quite often in the course of my work in juvenile court, I have heard a parent say, "I don't know how to control my 16-year-old child. He just does what he wants to do. What can I do?" An out-of-control 16-year-old is, in fact, a very difficult person with whom to deal. I usually answer such a parent with another question, "What did you do when he was two?" Most people in this situation admit that they did not do the things that must be done to raise responsible children. Sadly, this realization often comes too late to be of any real use to such parents and their children.

The episode of "Dinosaurs" mentioned above highlights the problem with early and preventative intervention by society in the lives of families. These attempts would be useless without a system of enforcement, and enforcement would involve unacceptable interference in a family's daily life. Even parents who recognize the need for help early in their child's life would undoubtedly resent having it forced upon them by the state.

A Passing Fad

Barry Feld, a professor of law at the University of Minnesota, says the rush to hold parents liable for their children's misdeeds is just one more in a long line of juvenile-justice fads. "The whole field of juvenile justice and simple-minded strategies to deal with complex problems," he says. "I know of no systemic evaluation that demonstrates the effectiveness of these statutes."

Laurel Shaper Walters, *Christian Science Monitor*, April 1, 1996.

The final problem with parental responsibility legislation is that the required parental behavior results only in adequate supervision of children, not necessarily in good parenting. My years of observing children have taught me that those children who receive consistent and loving guidance from a parent are the ones who rarely end up sitting at a table next to a lawyer in juvenile court. Of course, legislating love and concern is an impossible task, as is legislating responsibility. You cannot force parents to love, care for, and be responsible for their children. Love, concern, and responsibility are meaningless if they spring only from a need to comply with the law.

Mentor Programs

Even though parental responsibility laws are not a viable solution, there is a way that society can begin to combat the alarming increase in juvenile crime. That way has existed for many years and has proven successful. Rather than abandoning it in favor of punitive legislation, we should try to strengthen its effectiveness by using it more often. This method is the consistent and early involvement in the life of a potentially troubled child by a trained and caring adult volunteer.

Many mentoring programs that match willing adults to children at risk exist in this country. Programs like Big Brothers and Big Sisters of America have met with a great deal of success but continue to struggle with an insufficient number of adult volunteers. It is not difficult to identify children who are probable candidates for reckless and criminal conduct. The warning signs are visible to neighbors, relatives, teachers, and pastors. These people would be more likely to urge parents to use mentoring programs if they were readily available. These programs do not present the problems of parental responsibility laws. By their very nature, they concentrate on solutions and not punishment. They come into effect at a time when the assistance is most needed, and they are not coercive.

I have seen children who come from the most deplorable homes learn to live responsible lives because of the early intervention of one adult. It is surprising how little it takes to inculcate values into a young person. An adult who is willing to walk with a child, to answer a child's questions, and to provide an example of a life well led provides that child with a firm foundation. Moreover, the child learns that there is someone in this world who cares about him or her simply because of who he or she is. The child knows that the mentor's consistency in seeing him or her is neither based in a duty imposed by blood nor in an obligation arising from a job. The value placed on the child by the mentor is a mirror from which the child can see his or her own self-worth.

INTERFERENCE

There is another advantage to mentor programs. Occasionally, when I am dealing with a parent whose child has been brought into court, I am asked by that parent if I have any children. When the person learns that I do not, they often dismiss my advice. They reason that I know little or nothing about children that can be a benefit to them merely because I am not a parent. In some ways, they are correct. I have not experienced the trials of parenthood. It is not my place to stand on the sidelines and interfere with "other people's children."

For the same reason, parental responsibility laws are unlikely to succeed. Such laws are society's attempt to deal too late with other people's children from a comfortable distance. A mentor who walks with the child and the parents, on the other hand, cannot be dismissed so easily. Someone who is willing to spend time will be greeted more warmly by inadequate parents than the intruding police officer who walked into Earl Sinclair's kitchen.

"Curfews protect kids from other, dangerous kids."

GOVERNMENT-MANDATED TEEN CURFEWS ARE EFFECTIVE

San Diego Union-Tribune

In 1997, a federal appeals court struck down the teen curfew law in San Diego, California, as unconstitutionally vague. In the following viewpoint, the editors of the *San Diego Union-Tribune*, a daily newspaper, argue that the city should reimpose a curfew on teenagers that meets judicial guidelines. Juvenile crime dropped during curfew hours, the editors maintain; furthermore, curfews protect teens by keeping them home late at night when dangerous criminals are more likely to be on the streets.

As you read, consider the following questions:

1. In the author's opinion, what time should curfew be for teenagers on Friday and Saturday nights?
2. What were the Ninth Circuit Court of Appeals' objections to the current curfew law, as cited by the author?
3. What are the exceptions that would permit teens to be out past curfew, according to the *San Diego Union-Tribune*?

Reprinted, with permission, from "For Their Own Good: Curfew Protects Good Teens from Dangerous Ones," editorial, *San Diego Union-Tribune*, June 11, 1997.

S an Diego teens shouldn't get too comfortable with the idea that they can stay out late at night now that a federal appeals court has struck down the city's curfew law.

The city intends to come right back with a new law that will withstand legal challenge. The sooner the better.

FOR THEIR OWN GOOD

We understand that kids don't like fetters from the adult world. Rebelliousness is part of being a teen. However, as trite as this might sound, the curfew is for their own good.

Although 10 p.m. is too early on Friday and Saturday nights—it should be 11 p.m.—the concept of a curfew is sound. And it's legal. Many cities have curfews, including Dallas, whose law went all the way to the Supreme Court. After a federal appeals court upheld the law, the high court refused to reconsider it, letting the ruling stand.

The difference between the Dallas law and the San Diego law is that San Diego took a moribund 1947 law and started enforcing it in 1994. The City Council should have drafted a new one.

The court objected to the law's laundry list of things kids couldn't do after 10 p.m., saying it was too vague. The law states it's illegal for anyone under 18 to "loiter, idle, wander, stroll or play in or upon the public streets, highways, roads, alleys or other unsupervised places." Words like idle, wander and stroll are subject to many interpretations, the same as if the law inveighed against hanging out or kicking back.

Instead, according to a spokeswoman for City Attorney Casey Gwinn, the new law will simply say that kids can't be out after 10 p.m., unless they're with their parents, returning home from a supervised activity, coming from work or on an emergency errand.

That's patterned after the Dallas law. San Diego officials are not too concerned about comments made by judges from the 9th U.S. Circuit Court of Appeals who said the curfew violates parents' right to rear their children without undue government interference.

The U.S. Supreme Court had no such qualms when it refused to reconsider the Dallas law. Besides, many laws restrict kids from doing things adults are allowed to do.

CURFEWS WORK

Legalisms aside, the most important thing about curfew laws is that they work. And they protect kids. Curfews aren't a panacea for juvenile crime, but just another tool for law enforcement.

In San Diego, juvenile crime has dropped during curfew

hours. And more important, the number of juveniles who are victims of crime has dropped precipitously between 10 p.m. and daylight. The victims of juvenile crime usually are other juveniles. Curfews protect kids from other, dangerous kids.

JUVENILE CURFEWS

A sampling of the curfew laws in effect across the nation, the nighttime hours they are in effect, and the fines for violating the curfew.

Jurisdiction	Age	Weekdays	Weekend	Parental fines
Dallas	Under 17	11 to 6	12 to 6	Up to $500
Phoenix	15 & under	10 to 5	10 to 5	Up to $75
	16, 17	12 to 5	12 to 5	Up to $75
Chicago	Under 17	10:30 to 6	11 to 6	$200 to $500
New Orleans	Under 17	8 to 6 (Sept.–May) 9 to 6 (June–Aug.)	11 to 6	$500 and/or 60 hours of community service
Denver	Under 18	11 to 6	12 to 5	None*
North Little Rock, Ark.	Under 18	10 to 6	12 to 6	Fine for 2nd violation
Jacksonville, Fla.	Under 18	11 to 6	12 to 6	None

*Juveniles and parents who choose not to participate in an assigned diversion program or who fail to complete such a program may be assessed a fine.

Washington Times, June 17, 1996.

The 9th Circuit decision shouldn't deter elected officials in San Diego or anywhere else from enacting curfews. But officials must devise laws that aren't vague and provide for necessary exceptions. Curfews for teens are legal. The city of San Diego needs to make sure its new curfew follows standards set by other, court-tested laws.

| "At a time when many people are clamoring for less government, why pass curfew laws that usurp the rights of parents to raise their children as they see fit?"

GOVERNMENT–MANDATED TEEN CURFEWS ARE A MISTAKE

Geoffrey Canada

Geoffrey Canada argues in the following viewpoint that city-imposed teen curfews are a disturbing trend in crime prevention. He maintains that parents are a better judge than government officials of when their children should be home. Furthermore, Canada believes that enforcement of the curfew law by the police will lead to increased tensions between minority teenagers and the police. Canada is the president of the nonprofit youth group Rheedlen Centers for Children and Families and the author of *Fist, Stick, Knife, Gun*.

As you read, consider the following questions:

1. What determined whether the author was allowed to stay out late at night?
2. What times are children most likely to get into trouble, as cited by Canada?
3. In Canada's opinion, what should political leaders do to help teens and their families?

O ne reason I was able to grow up in the South Bronx of the 1950's and 1960's without getting into major trouble was that I lived under a curfew. The penalty for violating the curfew was swift and severe. Although I got to plead my case—a watch didn't work, the train was running late—the judge was seasoned and cynical (she had heard it all before). The usual verdict: guilty. The sentence: confinement to the apartment, when I wasn't at school, for a whole week.

This curfew was set, of course, by my mother, who raised four sons by herself. Like my mother, I am a strong believer in curfews. But I don't believe cities or states should impose them.

The calls for teen-age curfews by President Bill Clinton and Bob Dole and by Thomas V. Ognibene, a New York City Councilman, are part of a disturbing trend. Though New York doesn't have a curfew, most big cities now do. Increasingly, politicians are viewing the problems of youth solely through the prism of crime and punishment.

Indeed, while violent adult crime is falling in many big cities, youth crime and violence are generally on the rise. At the same time, the population of children in the 5- to 8-year-old range has risen by more than 20 percent over the past decade. So by the year 2005, the thinking goes, we may have an explosion of violence led by young people—including children who are being called "superpredators." The result: almost all proposals for young people involve "getting tough"—prosecuting juveniles as adults, for example.

THE PROBLEMS WITH CURFEWS

So what is wrong with official curfews? Many of the biggest American cities have them on the books. Dallas has reported that a curfew has helped reduce crime significantly. (No accurate data exist on the effectiveness of curfews nationwide.) But there are plenty of problems with curfews.

• *The wrong people impose them.* At a time when many people are clamoring for less government, why pass curfew laws that usurp the rights of parents to raise their children as they see fit? Families are a better context for kids to learn that freedoms come with responsibilities. Each year, I had to renegotiate my curfew with my mother; the older I got, the later the curfew. If there was a dance or a party, I got special permission from her, not the police, to stay out late. As a high school senior, I worked in a factory after classes and didn't get home until 11 P.M. My mother was skeptical about my ability to juggle work and school. But she gave me permission to try, with the proviso that if my grades dipped or I didn't get up on time, the job was over. My freedom to stay out late, for fun or work, depended on my maturity and on meeting the expectations of my mother and my teachers.

• *Curfews create a new category of criminal behavior.* These are tough times for young people. Guns claim thousands of their lives; schools are failing (some are even falling down). Jobs are hard to find in minority communities. Yet programs have been cut: summer employment, health and mental health services and after-school centers—even though children are more likely to get into trouble between 3 P.M. and 6 P.M. than at any other time, according to a report issued in 1995 by the National Center for Juvenile Justice. The last thing kids need is a new way to be negatively classified—as delinquent curfew-breakers.

A BURDEN ON PARENTS' RIGHTS

The curfew is, quite simply, an exercise of sweeping state control irrespective of parents' wishes. Without proper justification, it violates upon the fundamental right to rear children without undue interference. The ordinance is not a permissible "supportive" law, but rather an undue, adverse interference by the state.

Charles Wiggins, *Nunez v. San Diego*, June 9, 1997.

• *Curfews may worsen community problems with police and racism.* If you are a person of color and male, you invariably have a story to tell about police harassment or worse. I have my own stories. Will curfews be enforced uniformly? Many in the African-American and Latino communities doubt this. In New York City, police abuse in their neighborhoods includes the use of excessive force and the death of suspects in custody, according to an Amnesty International report issued in 1996.

A curfew won't work if adults do not support it because they think the police act unfairly. Besides, it puts police in a tough situation. Can you tell the difference between a 19-year-old (who may be exempt from a curfew) and a 17-year-old (who may not be)? A law that gives the police the right—indeed, requires them—to stop people on the basis of their perceived age, is an invitation to trouble.

I know that some parents need help with their children. I also know that when help is offered, parents respond. If political leaders really want to help, they should stop cutting resources for youth. Until then, if you want to know about curfews, before you talk to the President or a city councilman, talk to my mother.

PERIODICAL BIBLIOGRAPHY

The following articles have been selected to supplement the diverse views presented in this chapter. Addresses are provided for periodicals not indexed in the *Readers' Guide to Periodical Literature*, the *Alternative Press Index*, the *Social Sciences Index*, or the *Index to Legal Periodicals and Books*.

Craig Aaron	"Menaces to Society," *In These Times*, December 13, 1998.
David C. Anderson	"When Should Kids Go to Jail?" *American Prospect*, May/June 1998.
Pam Belluck	"Fighting Youth Crime, Some States Blend Adult and Juvenile Justice," *New York Times*, February 11, 1998.
Fox Butterfield	"Successes Reported for Curfews, but Doubts Persist," *New York Times*, June 3, 1996.
John J. DiIulio Jr.	"Jail Alone Won't Stop Juvenile Super-Predators," *Wall Street Journal*, June 11, 1997.
Evan Gahr	"Towns Turn Teens into Pumpkins," *Insight*, February 3, 1997. Available from 3600 New York Ave. NE, Washington, DC 20002.
Journal of Contemporary Criminal Justice	Entire issue on Prison and Jail Boot Camps, May 1997. Available from 2455 Teller Rd., Thousand Oaks, CA 91320.
Randall Kennedy	"Guilty by Association," *American Prospect*, May/June 1997.
Mark Langley	"My Son, the Teen-Age Predator," *Wall Street Journal*, April 2, 1996.
Joe Loconte	"Redd Scare," *Policy Review*, December 1996.
Abraham McLaughlin	"If Kids Get in Trouble, Parents May Feel Heat," *Christian Science Monitor*, February 17, 1998.
Tanya K. Metaksa	"Attacking Gangs, Not Civil Liberties," *American Rifleman*, December 1997. Available from 11250 Waples Mill Rd., Fairfax, VA 22030-9400.
Daniel J. Sharfstein	"Gangbusters," *American Prospect*, May/June 1997.
Nina Siegal	"Ganging Up on Civil Liberties," *Progressive*, October 1997.
Jill Smolowe	"Parenting on Trial," *Time*, May 20, 1996.
Gordon Witkin	"Colorado Has a New Brand of Tough Love," *U.S. News & World Report*, March 25, 1996.

CHAPTER 4

HOW CAN CRIME BE PREVENTED?

CHAPTER PREFACE

In October 1993, twelve-year-old Polly Klaas was kidnapped from her home in Petaluma, California. Two months later, Richard Allen Davis, a felon on parole who had served prison time for burglary and two kidnappings, confessed to Polly's kidnapping and subsequent murder. Outraged that Davis had been freed from prison despite his record, Polly's family worked to establish a "three strikes, you're out" law to keep criminals in prison and to deter those already convicted of one crime from committing another. The law requires that criminals convicted of their third violent felony receive a sentence of twenty-five years to life in prison. It also mandates that judges double the sentences for defendants who have one prior violent felony conviction. Five years after the passage of the three-strikes measure, however, opponents and supporters are still debating the effects of the law on the state's criminal justice system and crime rate.

Supporters of "three strikes" argue that the measure is responsible for reducing crime in the state. According to Bill Jones, California's secretary of state who wrote the three-strikes bill when he was an assemblyman, the overall crime rate in California fell nearly 38 percent between 1994 and 1998; the violent crime rate dropped 39.2 percent; and the state's homicide rate fell 51.5 percent in the same period. "We have had a million fewer crimes in California in the last five years," Jones said, "and that is what 'three strikes' is all about."

Opponents of the law contend, however, that "three strikes" is not necessarily responsible for the drop in the crime rate. A 1999 study by the Justice Policy Institute found that crime rates dropped just as much in states that do not have three-strikes laws and in California counties that did not vigorously prosecute criminals under the three-strikes law. Khaled Taqi-Eddin, a coauthor of the study, believes other factors may contribute to the drop in crime. "The economy is in the best shape it's been in years," he asserts. "There are a lot more jobs and a lot more people working," which means more potential criminals are gainfully employed.

While the three-strikes law has been politically popular, law enforcement, politicians, analysts, and the American public are unable to agree on its effectiveness in reducing crime. The use of the three-strikes law is among the issues examined by the authors in the following chapter on how to prevent crime.

| "Consistently when the number of executions goes down, the homicide rate goes up, and when the number of executions goes up, the homicide rate goes down."

THE DEATH PENALTY DETERS CRIME

Jay Johansen

According to Jay Johansen in the following viewpoint, the death penalty has a positive correlation to the homicide rate. As the number of executions declines, the homicide rate increases, and as the number of executions rises, the homicide rate falls. Therefore, Johansen concludes, the death penalty deters violent crime. Johansen is a freelance writer in Ohio.

As you read, consider the following questions:

1. According to the U.S. Department of Justice, what was the homicide rate throughout the 1950s, as cited by Johansen?
2. What happened in 1967, and how did this event affect the homicide rate, according to the author?
3. In Johansen's view, why did the Supreme Court once again permit executions to take place?

Reprinted from Jay Johansen, "Does Capital Punishment Deter Crime?" (March 1999) at www.infinet.com/~jayj/capdeter.htm, by permission of the author. (Footnotes in the original have been omitted in this reprint.)

A dvocates of capital punishment routinely argue that statistics prove that it deters crime. Opponents of capital punishment just as routinely argue that statistics prove that it does not.

I suppose a naive person might find this disagreement puzzling. Even if we cannot agree on moral questions, surely we could at least agree on basic facts. I mean, it would be understandable if an anti-capital punishment person said that, yes, it does deter crime, but it is still wrong because it is cruel and barbaric; or if a pro-capital punishment person said, okay, it doesn't deter crime any more than life imprisonment or some other punishment, but it is still right because it is just. But can't we at least agree on the underlying facts?

STATISTICS

But as I'm sure we're all aware these days, you can twist statistics to prove almost anything. Statisticians have developed many sophisticated techniques to carefully analyze data. People with a point to prove can abuse these techniques to distort the data.

But I'm a simple guy, so I decided to look at the simple statistics. Let's just look at the raw numbers: no clever analysis, no involved mathematical manipulation, just look at the numbers.

So, using statistics from the United States Department of Justice March 1998 website, here's my graph number 1: The homicide rate for each year since 1950. The rate is given as the number of homicides for every million people.

GRAPH 1: HOMICIDE RATE

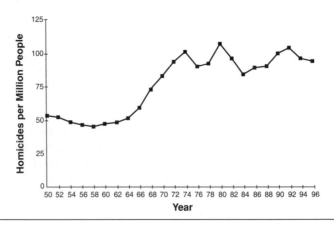

A casual glance at this graph clearly shows that homicide rates increased sharply beginning about 1965 or 1966, they took a steep dive from 1980 to 1985, started back up again until 1991–1992, and now appear to be inching down.

Surely a reasonable, concerned person could ask if there is any apparent cause for the sudden sharp increase in the late 60's. And surely we could look with hope at the drop in the early 80's, and ask if there was not something that was happening then that we could reproduce.

So let's look at another graph. Graph number 2 shows the homicide rate, just as above, and on top of this I show the number of cases where capital punishment was imposed.

GRAPH 2: HOMICIDE RATE VS EXECUTIONS

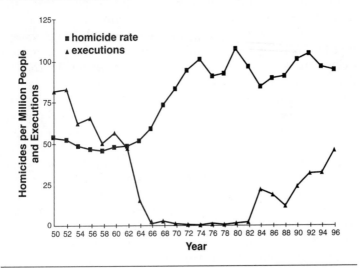

Note the interesting correlations. The number of executions plummeted from 47 in 1962 to 2 in 1967 to zero in 1968. The homicide rate, which had been holding steady around 50 throughout the 50's, started up in 1965, just two years after executions began their plummet. The biggest increase in one year came in 1967, the same year that the last person was executed.

So okay, maybe this was simply a coincidence. Capital punishment was reinstated a decade later. What happened then?

In 1976 the Supreme Court issued several decisions in which they basically backtracked and again allowed capital punishment. (They didn't quite say that they were changing their minds or admitting error, but rather that the flaws which they had discovered in the previous capital punishment laws had now been corrected.) The first person was actually executed in 1977.

In the very year of these Supreme Court decisions, the homicide rate plummeted. But no more than two people were actually executed in any one year through 1982, and so perhaps criminals concluded that the danger of execution was remote, and the homicide rate crawled back up. Then the number of executions suddenly went up in 1983, and in that year the homicide rate showed its biggest one-year drop. With the sudden surge in executions in 1996, the homicide rate again fell.

A Mirror Image

Indeed, just looking at this graph we can see that the homicide rate is almost the mirror image of the number of executions. Consistently when the number of executions goes down, the homicide rate goes up, and when the number of executions goes up, the homicide rate goes down. The only major exception to this is the fall in homicides in 1976, which came *before* executions re-started. But this is easily explainable by the fact that the court decisions allowing executions to resume came a year or two before executions actually did resume. Criminals may have been responding to press reports that capital punishment was once again going to take place, in advance of it actually happening.

I'm sure that opponents of capital punishment will say that my analysis here is too simplistic; that I have failed to take other factors into account; that this correlation between execution rates and homicide rates is pure coincidence, and that other factors explain why homicide rates went up and down at these times that had nothing to do with the number of executions.

To which I reply, Well, maybe, but I think you have an awfully hard sell. If there was just one point of correlation, it might be explained by coincidence. That is, if the homicide rate had gone up when capital punishment was abolished, but when capital punishment was re-instated the homicide rate had remained unchanged, or had gone up further, one might reasonably say that the first correlation was simply coincidence. But when we can clearly see that the two numbers mirror each other, consistently over a period of almost fifty years, attributing this to coincidence gets pretty hard to believe.

The obvious conclusion from looking at the statistics, without any fancy "analysis" or "factoring out of other factors," is that capital punishment *does* deter murder.

"The death penalty is not just useless—it is positively harmful and diverts resources from genuine crime control measures."

THE DEATH PENALTY DOES NOT DETER CRIME

Eric M. Freedman

The death penalty not only does not deter violent crime, but actually works against reducing the crime rate, argues Eric M. Freedman in the following viewpoint. States that use the death penalty have crime rates that are nearly indistinguishable from those states that do not have the death penalty, he contends. Furthermore, criminal cases in which the death penalty is sought are much more expensive to investigate and try, he maintains, thus denying much-needed funds to programs that have been proven to reduce crime. Freedman teaches courses on constitutional law and the death penalty at Hofstra University School of Law in Hempstead, New York.

As you read, consider the following questions:

1. What evidence does the author present to support his contention that the death penalty does not deter crime?
2. According to Freedman, why are death penalty cases and trials so much more expensive than cases in which the punishment is life imprisonment?
3. In what way is the death penalty discriminatory, in Freedman's opinion?

Excerpted from Eric M. Freedman, "The Case Against the Death Penalty," *USA Today* magazine, March 1997. Reprinted by permission of the Society for the Advancement of Education; ©1997.

On September 1, 1995, New York rejoined the ranks of states imposing capital punishment. Although the first death sentence has yet to be imposed, an overwhelming factual record from around the country makes the consequence of this action easily predictable: New Yorkers will get less crime control than they had before.

Anyone whose public policy goals are to provide a criminal justice system that delivers swift, accurate, and evenhanded results—and to reduce the number of crimes that actually threaten most people in their daily lives—should be a death penalty opponent. The reason is simple: The death penalty not only is useless in itself, but counterproductive to achieving those goals. It wastes enormous resources—fiscal and moral—on a tiny handful of cases, to the detriment of measures that might have a significant impact in improving public safety.

NOT A DETERRENT

Those who believe the death penalty somehow is an emotionally satisfying response to horrific crimes should ask themselves whether they wish to adhere to that initial reaction in light of the well-documented facts:

Fact: The death penalty does not reduce crime. Capital punishment proponents sometimes assert that it simply is logical to think that the death penalty is a deterrent. Whether or not the idea is logical, it is not true, an example of the reality that many intuitively obvious propositions—e.g., that a heavy ball will fall faster if dropped from the Leaning Tower of Pisa than a light one—are factually false.

People who commit capital murders generally do not engage in probability analysis concerning the likelihood of getting the death penalty if they are caught. They may be severely mentally disturbed people like Ted Bundy, who chose Florida for his final crimes *because* it had a death penalty.

Whether one chooses to obtain data from scholarly studies, the evidence of long-term experience, or accounts of knowledgeable individuals, he or she will search in vain for empirical support for the proposition that imposing the death penalty cuts the crime rate. Instead, that person will find:

• The question of the supposed deterrent effect of capital punishment is perhaps the single most studied issue in the social sciences. The results are as unanimous as scholarly studies can be in finding the death penalty not to be a deterrent.

• Eighteen of the 20 states with the highest murder rates have and use the death penalty. Of the nation's 20 big cities with the highest murder rates, 17 are in death penalty jurisdictions. Between 1975 and 1985, almost twice as many law enforcement officers were killed in death penalty states as in non–death penalty states. Over nearly two decades, the neighboring states of Michigan, with no death penalty, and Indiana, which regularly imposes death sentences and carries out executions, have had virtually indistinguishable homicide rates.

• Myron Love, the presiding judge in Harris County, Texas (which includes Houston), the county responsible for 10% of all executions in the entire country since 1976, admits that "We are not getting what I think we should be wanting and that is to deter crime. . . . In fact, the result is the opposite. We're having more violence, more crime."

An Expensive Punishment

Fact: The death penalty is extraordinarily expensive. Contrary to popular intuition, a system with a death penalty is vastly more expensive than one where the maximum penalty is keeping murderers in prison for life. A 1982 New York study estimated the death penalty cost conservatively at three times that of life imprisonment, the ratio that Texas (with a system that is on the brink of collapse due to underfunding) has experienced. In Florida, each execution runs the state $3,200,000—six times the expense of life imprisonment. California has succeeded in executing just two defendants (one a volunteer) since 1976, but could save about $90,000,000 *per year* by abolishing the death penalty and re-sentencing all of its Death Row inmates to life.

In response, it often is proposed to reduce the costs by eliminating "all those endless appeals in death penalty cases." This is not a new idea. In recent years, numerous efforts have been made on the state and Federal levels to do precisely that. Their failure reflects some simple truths:

• Most of the extra costs of the death penalty are incurred prior to and at trial, not in postconviction proceedings. Trials are far more likely under a death penalty system (since there is so little incentive to plea-bargain). They have two separate phases (unlike other trials) and typically are preceded by special motions and extra jury selection questioning—steps that, if not taken before trial, most likely will result in the eventual reversal of the conviction.

• Much more investigation usually is done in capital cases, particularly by the prosecution. In New York, for instance, the office of the State Attorney General (which generally does not participate in local criminal prosecutions) is creating a new multi-lawyer unit to provide support to county district attorneys in capital cases.

• These expenses are incurred even though the outcome of most such trials is a sentence other than death and even though up to 50% of the death verdicts that are returned are reversed on the constitutionally required first appeal. Thus, the taxpayers foot the bill for all the extra costs of capital pretrial and trial proceedings and then must pay either for incarcerating the prisoner for life or the expenses of a retrial, which itself often leads to a life sentence. In short, even if all postconviction proceedings following the first appeal were abolished, the death penalty system still would be more expensive than the alternative. . . .

OTHER PROGRAMS SUFFER

Fact: The death penalty actually reduces public safety. The costs of the death penalty go far beyond the tens of millions of dollars wasted in the pursuit of a chimera. The reality is that, in a time of fixed or declining budgets, those dollars are taken away from a range of programs that would be beneficial. For example:

• New York State, due to financial constraints, can not provide bulletproof vests for every peace officer—a project that, unlike the death penalty, certainly would save law enforcement lives.

• According to FBI statistics, the rate at which murders are solved has dropped to an all-time low. Yet, empirical studies consistently demonstrate that, as with other crimes, the murder rate decreases as the probability of detection increases. Putting money into investigative resources, rather than wasting it on the death penalty, could have a significant effect on crime.

• Despite the large percentage of ordinary street crimes that are narcotics-related, the states lack the funding to permit drug treatment on demand. The result is that people who are motivated to cure their own addictions are relegated to supporting themselves through crime, while the money that could fund treatment programs is poured down the death penalty drain.

DISCRIMINATION

Fact: The death penalty is arbitrary in operation. Any reasonably conscientious supporter of the death penalty surely would agree with the proposition that, before someone is executed by the state, he or she first should receive the benefits of a judicial process that is as fair as humanly possible.

However, the one thing that is clear about the death penalty system that actually exists—as opposed to the idealized one some capital punishment proponents assume to exist—is that it does not provide a level of fairness which comes even close to equaling the gravity of the irreversible sanction being imposed. This failure of the system to function even reasonably well when it should be performing excellently breeds public cynicism as to how satisfactorily the system runs in ordinary, non-capital cases.

CAPITAL PUNISHMENT IS NOT THE ANSWER

We believe that the state must protect the people and discipline those who commit serious crimes against them. The question is how best to do this. In recent years many thoughtful people have concluded that capital punishment is not the answer:

• The death penalty does not effectively deter serious crime in our nation.

• The death penalty does not alleviate the fear of violent crime or better safeguard the people.

• The death penalty does not protect society more effectively than other alternatives such as life imprisonment without parole.

• The death penalty does not restore the social order breached by offenders.

• The death penalty is not imposed with fairness, falling disproportionately on racial and ethnic minorities and the poor.

• The death penalty is not imposed in such a way as to prevent the execution of innocent death-row inmates.

Deacons of the Diocese of Paterson, N.J., *Origins*, January 21, 1999.

That reaction, although destructive, is understandable, because the factors that are significant in determining whether or not a particular defendant receives a death sentence have nothing at all to do with the seriousness of his or her crime. The key variables, rather, are:

• Racial discrimination in death-sentencing, which has been documented repeatedly. . . .

Many . . . studies, whose validity have been confirmed in a major analysis for Congress by the General Accounting Office, . . . uniformly have found that, even when all other factors are held constant, the races of the victim and defendant are critical variables in determining who is sentenced to death.

Thus, black citizens are the victim of double discrimination. From initial charging decisions to plea bargaining to jury sentencing, they are treated more harshly when they are defendants, but their lives are given less value when they are victims. Moreover, all-white or virtually all-white juries still are commonplace in many places.

One common reaction to this evidence is not to deny it, but to attempt to evade the facts by taking refuge in the assertion that any effective system for guarding against racial discrimination would mean the end of the death penalty. Such a statement is a powerful admission that governments are incapable of running racially neutral capital punishment systems. The response of any fair-minded person should be that, if such is the case, governments should not be running capital punishment systems.

• Income discrimination. Most capital defendants can not afford an attorney, so the court must appoint counsel. Every major study of this issue, including those of the Powell Commission appointed by Chief Justice William Rehnquist, the American Bar Association, the Association of the Bar of the City of New York, and innumerable scholarly journals, has found that the quality of defense representation in capital murder trials generally is far lower than in felony cases.

The field is a highly specialized one, and since the states have failed to pay the amounts necessary to attract competent counsel, there is an overwhelming record of poor people being subjected to convictions and death sentences that equally or more culpable—but more affluent—defendants would not have suffered.

• Mental disability. Jurors are more likely to sentence to death people who seem different from themselves than individuals who seem similar to themselves. That is the reality underlying the stark fact that those with mental disabilities are sentenced to death at a rate far higher than can be justified by any neutral explanation. This reflects prejudice, pure and simple.

INNOCENT PEOPLE ARE EXECUTED

Fact: Capital punishment inevitably will be inflicted on the innocent. It is ironic that, just as New York was reinstating the death penalty, it was in the midst of a convulsive scandal involving the widespread fabrication of evidence by the New York State Police that had led to scores of people—including some innocent ones—being convicted and sentenced to prison terms. Miscarriages of justice unquestionably will occur in any human system, but the death penalty presents two special problems in this regard:

• The arbitrary factors discussed above have an enormous negative impact on accuracy. In combination with the emotional atmosphere generally surrounding capital cases, they lead to a situation where the truth-finding process in capital cases is less reliable than in others. Indeed, a 1993 House of Representatives subcommittee report found 48 instances over the previous two decades in which innocent people had been sentenced to death.

• The stark reality is that death is final. A mistake can not be corrected if the defendant has been executed.

How often innocent people have been executed is difficult to quantify; once a defendant has been executed, few resources generally are devoted to the continued investigation of the case. Nonetheless, within the past few years, independent investigations by major news organizations have uncovered three cases, two in Florida and one in Mississippi, where people were put to death for crimes they did not commit. Over time, others doubtless will come to light (while still others will remain undiscovered), but it will be too late.

The fact that the system sometimes works—for those who are lucky enough to obtain somehow the legal and investigative resources or media attention necessary to vindicate their claims of innocence—does not mean that most innocent people on Death Row are equally fortunate. Moreover, many Death Row inmates who have been exonerated would have been executed if the legal system had moved more quickly. . . .

The death penalty is not just useless—it is positively harmful and diverts resources from genuine crime control measures. Arbitrarily selecting out for execution not the worst criminals, but a racially determined handful of the poorest, most badly represented, least mentally healthy, and unluckiest defendants—some of whom are innocent—breeds cynicism about the entire criminal justice system.

Thus, the Criminal Justice Section of the New York State Bar Association—which includes prosecutors, judges, and defense attorneys—opposed re-institution of the death penalty because of "the enormous cost associated with such a measure, and the serious negative impact on the delivery of prosecution and defense services throughout the state that will result." Meanwhile, Chief Justice Dixon of the Louisiana Supreme Court put it starkly: "Capital punishment is destroying the system."

> "'Three strikes' incapacitates active
> criminals, who can no longer
> commit crimes against the public."

"THREE-STRIKES" LAWS PREVENT CRIME

Dan Lungren

Many states have implemented a "three-strikes" law in which criminals receive mandatory sentences for their first and second crimes; criminals convicted of a third violent felony are sent to prison for life. In the following viewpoint, former California attorney general Dan Lungren argues that the three-strikes law is a fair and effective approach to combating crime. The law is responsible for the state's declining crime rate, he maintains, because it forces criminals to choose between giving up a life of crime and spending the rest of their lives in prison.

As you read, consider the following questions:

1. What facet of sentencing is still left to the judge's discretion, according to Lungren?
2. What are the objections to three-strikes laws, according to the law's opponents?
3. According to the author, how did the migratory patterns of criminals change once California passed its three-strikes law?

Excerpted from Dan Lungren, "Three Cheers for Three Strikes: California Enjoys Record Drop in Crime," at www.nonline.com/procon/html/3strikes_pro.html. Reprinted with permission.

Crime in California is dropping—fast. So far, the 1990s look to be the most promising for reducing crime since the state started keeping complete statistics in 1952. Although California suffered—along with the rest of the nation—while the crime rate nearly quadrupled between 1960 and 1980, California is now recording some of the largest crime reductions of any state.

A Dramatic Reduction in Crime

Preliminary crime statistics for 1995 show that the overall crime rate in California fell 8.5 percent; violent crimes dropped 5.5 percent and property crimes fell 10.1 percent. If the trend holds, California will record a third straight year of falling crime in 1996, including a marked acceleration in 1995 and 1996. The hard evidence points to historic decreases in all categories of crime in the state. California is about to set state records for:

- The largest one-year drop in state history in the rate and number of crimes;
- The largest two-year decline in the number of crimes;
- The first two-year drop in all major categories of crime (homicide, rape, robbery, aggravated assault, burglary, and motor-vehicle theft);
- The largest one-year drop in the number of violent crimes;
- The largest one-year drop in the rate and number of property crimes;
- The largest one-year drop in the number of burglaries;
- The largest one-year drop in the number of motor-vehicle thefts.

What accounts for these astonishing numbers? I would suggest it is in large part due to California's passage of a "three strikes and you're out" law, which has done more to stop revolving-door justice than any other measure in state or federal law. Enacted in 1994 by both popular initiative and legislative action, the law requires a defendant convicted of a felony to serve an indeterminate life sentence when it is proved that he has committed two or more previous felonies defined as "violent" or "serious." Offenders given a life sentence become eligible for parole only after serving 25 years or three times the term that the current conviction would ordinarily warrant, whichever is greater. A "two strikes" provision, part of the same law, requires that when a defendant is convicted of a felony, and has been previously convicted of one "serious or violent" felony, the term of imprisonment is twice the usual sentence provided for the second felony conviction.

In June 1996, the California Supreme Court held in *People v.*

Romero that, notwithstanding the ostensible mandatory language of the "three strikes" law, judges retain the discretion to strike or dismiss prior felony convictions; the court's judgment relied on statutory interpretation and the separation of powers. Thus, the state of the law is that while judges have discretion to strike a prior conviction, our district attorneys will still prove prior felony convictions and state courts will still sentence offenders under "three strikes." I have sponsored legislation to narrowly define and restrict the discretion that judges will have in these cases.

ACCOUNTABILITY FOR CRIMINAL CHOICES

As written and applied, "three strikes" is a model of strict and even-handed justice. It demands accountability, reflects common sense, presents a clear and certain penalty, and uncompromisingly invests in public safety. I like to reflect on former Chief Justice Warren Burger's comments made before an American Bar Association meeting in 1981: "A far greater factor is the deterrent effect of swift and certain consequences: swift arrest, prompt trial, certain penalty and—at some point—finality of judgment." Can anybody believe otherwise? The quotation reflects the chief justice's fundamental understanding that the rule of law affords the complementary blessings of both freedom and responsibility and provides the governing framework in which individual citizens make their individual decisions. The rule of law protects our free will from arbitrary constraints; at the same time, it provides consistency and impartiality to the life of the state and its citizens. What seems obvious in this formula is that as individuals exercise their individual, personal liberties in living their lives and in interacting with others, they also become personally accountable for the choices they make—choices from which clear consequences arise.

Yet, many opponents of "three strikes" disagree with the notion of strict personal accountability. Of course, while most of the self-proclaimed experts in criminal justice state their objections on other grounds—they call "three strikes" draconian, ineffective, too broad, too tough, and too expensive—the real theme that resounds in their criticism is that "three strikes" "revictimizes" persons who already have been "victimized" by the forces of an unfriendly society and an adversarial government. In short, their view is that the targets of "three strikes" are not accountable for their conduct because "complex" forces extrinsic to the individual are the principal causes of criminal activity: poor education, unemployment, a detrimental social situation, or even the law enforcement system. Further, these critics have employed this philosophy to demand that sentencing for convicted criminals be made in light of "mitigating circumstances" and that incarceration should be for "rehabilitative purposes" to redress what society "did" to the inmate.

The voters of California have rejected this nonsense. And the record shows "three strikes" is doing precisely what the voters demanded when they overwhelmingly passed the initiative, by 72 percent to 28. The career criminal with multiple serious or violent felony convictions is being forced to make what should be an easy decision: Either stop committing felonies and live the remainder of your life in freedom, or spend 25 years to life in prison the next time you are caught and convicted of a felony. The career criminal will be held personally accountable for his decisions. Imagine that! When the voters rejected revolving-door justice, they rejected the arguments of apologists that we can divorce negative personal conduct from individual accountability.

PROPORTIONAL PUNISHMENT

The second criticism against "three strikes" by criminal apologists is that the law does not furnish proportionate punishment. These critics focus on the cases in which a habitual felon is charged with a "minor" property or drug offense that qualifies as a third strike. They allege it is wholly improper to impose an indeterminate life sentence for a "minor" crime and that instead the offender should be given special consideration or more lenient treatment. The philosophical approach advocated here is that criminal conduct should be viewed in isolation of past history and surrounding circumstances. If a habitual felon currently commits a crime that is classified as a felony under California law, and he has convictions for two previous "serious" felonies, is it any surprise that Californians want a tougher punishment for the current felony?

Let's examine what constitutes a "serious or violent felony" for a "three strikes" prior conviction: murder or voluntary manslaughter; mayhem; rape; sodomy by force, violence, duress, menace, threat of great bodily injury, or fear of immediate and unlawful bodily injury on the victim or another person; oral copulation by force, violence, duress, et cetera; lewd or lascivious acts on children; felonies with personal use of firearm; attempted murder; assault with intent to commit rape or robbery; assault with deadly weapon; arson; kidnapping; selling drugs to minors; and many others. If these are not "serious" enough, I would like to know which ones should be dropped as insufficiently serious. When the third strike is but a "minor" felony, such as grand theft or possession of certain drugs for sale, why should society ignore the habit-ual criminal activity of this offender when sentencing him?

Common sense dictates the answer to this question. First, so-ciety does not view crime in a vacuum. As Princeton professor John DiIulio wrote, "Most Americans rightly think in terms of total criminality—the full social and moral weight of an of-fender's acts against life, liberty, and property. They reject the criminological equivalent of grade inflation—judging plea-bargained-gorged prisoners by their last conviction rather than their overall criminal grade-point average, adult and juvenile." Second, an offender who has committed a series of violent or serious crimes is likely to commit additional crimes of the same nature; wisdom demands that an offender's criminal record be the starting point for determining punishment. Finally, the rule of law demands a response to a lifestyle of destruction and vio-lence. There is nothing disproportionate about giving a harsh sentence to a felon who has not learned from having committed two serious felonies before.

DETERRENCE EFFECT

There has been a marked split of opinion, at least in academia, as to how best to prevent crime. On the one hand, some argue that habitual criminal activity can be "cured" by placing offend-ers in correctional programs that renounce retributive goals and instead stress the redemptive value of education, vocational in-struction, and even group therapy. Another school of thought centers on the positive behavioral effects of a system of clear and certain consequences for destructive and criminal behavior. Unfortunately, many in the "redemptive programs" group reject outright the legitimacy of deterrence. The causes of criminal be-havior are far too complex, they say, to permit any generaliza-tions about whether individuals will consider legal prohibitions or sanctions when they act and interact in society—especially when they are hungry, ill-housed, under-educated, or emotion-ally neglected.

The value of deterrence, however, is grossly underestimated by these "experts," who have devised no way to prove or dis-prove its effects. I believe certainty of incarceration, for a long and inevitable period, nonetheless has a dramatic effect on the behavior of individuals. Consider the statement of a veteran homicide detective in the Sacramento police department as to the law's impact: "You hear [the criminals] talking about it all the time. These guys are really squirming. They know what's go-ing on. . . . I've flipped 100 percent." Gregory Gaines had just been released from Folsom State Prison with two serious or violent felony convictions—two "strikes"—and told a *Sacramento Bee* reporter that many other inmates have decided to heed the warnings of the "three strikes" law. "It's a brand-new me, mainly because of the law. It's going to keep me working, keep my attitude adjusted."

Jerry Barnett for the *Indianapolis News*. Reprinted by permission.

Perhaps the most interesting statistics track the migratory patterns of felons on parole in California. In the last year before "three strikes" became law in 1994, 226 more paroled felons chose to move to California than moved out. After "three strikes" took effect, the flow reversed: 1,335 more paroled felons chose to leave California in 1995 than to enter. We've gone from being a net importer of paroled felons to a net exporter! Coincidence? Hardly. . . .

ZERO TOLERANCE

Some critics of "three strikes" argue that the example of New York City, which has enjoyed a steep drop in crime without the benefit of state laws similar to California's, undercuts the case for "three strikes" policies. New York City, however, invested in a comprehensive community-oriented policing program along with a "zero tolerance" policy that requires officers to strictly enforce every possible violation. Like "three strikes," New York City's program costs money—and it works. (New York City has added 7,000 officers since 1990. The entire Los Angeles Police Department totals 8,737; New York City 37,800.) Ironically, it is deterrence again at work in New York City—the criminals in the city know the police are there and change their behavior accordingly.

Unfortunately, we are told that a proportionally large group of young males, currently in their pre-teen years, will soon move into their "crime-prone" years. We should refuse to accept the notion that a high rate of crime will be committed by these youths. A juvenile crime wave is not inevitable, just as our high crime rates of the past were not inevitable. As a society we have to confront the conditions that exacerbate levels of juvenile crime and violence. Our challenge is to implement juvenile crime laws and policies which will deter as many as possible from a life of crime while still incarcerating those teenagers who commit serious violence on our citizens. There is an important place for prevention and intervention programs for our young.

Although "three strikes" will incarcerate more habitual criminals, the costs are justified. The price of allowing these offenders to return to a lifestyle of victimizing citizens is too high. "Three strikes" incapacitates active criminals, who can no longer commit crimes against the public. "Three strikes" removes from our streets the harmful role models these offenders present to our youth and to gang "wannabes." "Three strikes" re-introduces into our collective consciousness a moral imperative that criminal activity should not be tolerated in any way. Most importantly, "three strikes" reduces crime by providing a solid and unquestionable deterrent to criminal behavior. California's sharp decline in crime in 1995 and 1996 may be attributable to numerous, complex factors, but it is indisputable that "three strikes" has played a major role in reshaping public safety in California, both for law-abiding citizens and for would-be criminals.

"Demographics (i.e., fewer young men) and better policing are more responsible for the dropping crime rate than criminals' fear of mandatory minimums."

"THREE-STRIKES" LAWS ARE UNFAIR

John Cloud

"Three-strikes" laws, which impose mandatory prison terms for drug crimes and felonies, are unfair, ineffective, and extremely costly, argues John Cloud in the following viewpoint. Imprisoning young first-time offenders only ensures that their role models are hardened, older criminals, he asserts. Furthermore, criminologists maintain that better policing and a declining population of young men are responsible for the falling crime rate, not mandatory sentences. Cloud is a staff writer for *Time* magazine.

As you read, consider the following questions:
1. Why did Marc Klaas change his mind about the validity of three-strikes laws, according to Cloud?
2. Where did the funds for New York's prison construction boom come from, in Cloud's opinion?
3. Which states are beginning to change their laws concerning mandatory minimum sentences, as cited by the author?

Remember little Polly Klaas? She was the 12-year-old Petaluma, California, girl whisked from a slumber party in 1993 and found murdered two months later. Her father Marc, horrified to learn that her killer was on parole and had attacked children in the past, called for laws making parole less common. He joined with others backing a "three strikes and you're out" law for California—no parole, ever, for those convicted of three felonies. Klaas went on TV, got in the papers, met the President—all within weeks after his daughter's body was found.

Then he began studying how the three-strikes law would actually work. He noticed that a nonviolent crime—burglary, for instance—could count as a third strike. "That meant you could get life for breaking into someone's garage and stealing a stereo," he says. "I've had my stereo stolen, and I've had my daughter stolen. I believe I know the difference."

Klaas began speaking against three strikes. But his daughter had already become a symbol for the crackdown on crime, and California's legislature passed the three-strikes law. It now seems politically untouchable, despite horror stories like the one about a Los Angeles 27-year-old who got 25 years to life for stealing pizza. Last year [1998] two state senators tried to limit the measure to violent crimes, but the bill didn't make it out of committee. Governor Pete Wilson vetoed a bill simply to study the effects of the law.

Wilson probably knew what the study would conclude: while three-strikes laws sound great to the public, they aren't working. A growing number of states and private groups have scrutinized these and other "mandatory-minimum laws," the generic name for statutes forcing judges to impose designated terms. The studies are finding that the laws cost enormous amounts of money, largely to lock up such nonviolent folks as teenage drug couriers, dope-starved addicts and unfortunate offenders like the Iowa man who got 10 years for stealing $30 worth of steaks from a grocery store and then struggling with a store clerk who tackled him (the struggle made it a felony).

How much are we spending? Put it this way: mandatory minimums are the reason so many prisons are booming in otherwise impoverished rural counties across America. The U.S. inmate population has more than doubled (to nearly 2 million) since the mid-'80s, when mandatory sentencing became the hot new intoxicant for politicians. New York (the first state to enact mandatory minimums) has sloshed $600 million into prison construction since 1988; not coincidentally, in the same period it has sliced $700 million from higher education. Americans will have to spend even more in the future to house and treat all the aging inmates. California has already filled its 114,000 prison beds, and double-bunks 46,000 additional inmates.

More important, mandatory minimums for nonviolent (and arguably victimless) drug crimes insult justice. Most mandatory sentences were designed as weapons in the drug war, with an awful consequence: we now live in a country where it's common to get a longer sentence for selling a neighbor a joint than for, say, sexually abusing her. (According to a 1997 federal report, those convicted of drug trafficking have served an average of almost seven years, nearly a year longer than those convicted of sexual abuse.) Several . . . books, including Michael Massing's The Fix, point out that the tough-on-drugs policies of the past 15 years haven't had much impact on the heart of the drug problem, abuse by long-term urban addicts. Even the usually hard-line drug czar Barry McCaffrey has written that "we can't incarcerate our way out of the drug problem." He has urged Congress to reduce mandatory minimums for crack, which are currently 100 times as heavy as those for powdered coke and impact most on minority youth.

This injustice is most palpable on city streets. In places like New York there are more black and Hispanic kids in prison than in college. That injustice may have played a role in the fate of Derrick Smith, a New York City youth who in October [1998] faced a sentence of 15 years to life for selling crack. At the sentence hearing a distraught Smith told the judge, "I'm only 19. This is terrible." He then hurled himself out of a courtroom window and fell 16 stories to his death. "He didn't kill anyone; he didn't rob anyone," says his mother. "This happened because we are black and poor."

Worst of all, mandatory minimums have done little to solve the problems for which they were crafted. Casual drug use has declined since the 1970s, but the size of the addict population has remained stable. And even conservative criminologists concede that demographics (i.e., fewer young men) and better policing are more responsible for the dropping crime rate than criminals' fear of mandatory minimums. John DiIulio Jr., the Princeton professor who wrote a 1994 defense of mandatory sentencing for the Wall Street Journal with the charming headline LET 'EM ROT, now opposes mandatory minimums for drug crimes. He points out that more and more young, nonviolent, first-time offenders are being incarcerated—"and they won't find suitable role models in prison."

But even some older, repeat offenders are getting punishments that seem ridiculously disproportionate to their crimes. Consider Douglas Gray, a husband, father, Vietnam veteran and owner of a roofing business who bought a pound of marijuana in an Alabama motel for $900 several years ago. The seller turned out to be a police informant, a felon fresh from prison whom cops paid $100 to do the deal. Because Gray had been arrested for several petty crimes 13 years earlier—crimes that didn't even carry a prison sentence—he fell under the state's "habitual offender" statutes. He got life without parole.

CALIFORNIA'S "THREE-STRIKES" LAW IS A FAILURE

Using data from the California Department of Corrections and the California Department of Justice, this study examined the relative effect of California's "Three Strikes" law on different . . . jurisdictions. . . .

• County-by-county comparisons showed that counties that vigorously and strictly enforced the "Three Strikes" law did not experience a decline in any crime category relative to more lenient counties. Data reveal that the highest sentencing counties are invoking the law at rates 3 to 12 times higher than the lowest counties.

• The seven-fold proportionally greater use of three strikes in Sacramento and Los Angeles was not associated with a bigger crime decline than Alameda and San Francisco counties that rarely invoke the law.

• San Francisco, the county which uses "Three Strikes" most sparingly, witnessed a greater decline in violent crime, homicides, and all index crime than the six heaviest enforcing counties.

Mike Males, Dan Macallair, and Khaled Taqi-Eddin, Justice Policy Institute executive summary of *Striking Out*, March 1999.

The good news is that a consensus is emerging among judges (including Reagan-appointee Chief Justice William Rehnquist), law enforcers and crime experts—among them many conservatives who once supported the laws—that mandatory minimums are foolish. The Supreme Court . . . declined to hear a case challenging the California three-strikes law, but four Justices expressed concern about the law's effect and seemed to invite other challenges. A few brave politicians have gingerly suggested that the laws may be something we should rethink. Some states are starting to backtrack on tough sentencing laws:

• *Michigan* Last February [1998] former Republican Governor William Milliken called the "650 Lifer Law" his biggest mistake.

The 1978 law mandated a life-without-parole term for possession with intent to deliver at least 650 g (about 1.4 lbs.) of heroin or cocaine. But though the law was intended to net big fish, few major dealers got hit. In fact, 86% of the "650 lifers" had never done time; 70% were poor. "A lot of them were young people who made very stupid mistakes but shouldn't have to pay for it for the rest of their lives," says state representative Barbara Dobb, the Republican who began a reform effort. In August, G.O.P. Governor John Engler signed a law allowing 650 lifers to be paroled after 15 years.

• *Utah* In March 1995, Republican senate president Lane Beattie, concerned about the excesses of mandatory minimums, introduced a bill to eliminate them in certain cases. Worried about the political fallout, he did so near midnight on the last day of the legislative session. The bill passed quietly, without debate, but victims' groups noticed. Though a public outcry followed, the G.O.P. Governor said he agreed with the bill and refused to veto it.

• *Georgia* In the final minutes of the 1996 legislative session, state lawmakers nixed mandatory life sentences for second-time drug offenders. State statistics showed that four-fifths of those serving life had hawked less than $50 in narcotics. Even state prosecutors backed the change.

• *New York* John Dunne, a former Republican legislator who helped devise the Rockefeller Drug Laws, the mandatory-sentencing legislation promulgated in the 1970s by Governor Nelson Rockefeller, is lobbying to end them. "This was a good idea 25 years ago, but the sad experience is that it has not had an effect," says Dunne, who also served in the Bush Administration. "Behind closed doors, virtually everyone will say these drug laws are not working, but they cannot say that publicly."

Certainly no one in Washington is saying it publicly. The House Judiciary Committee didn't even hold hearings on the bill that created the current minimums, which coasted to victory just in time for the 1986 midterm elections. [In 1998] Congress and the President added a new mandatory minimum to the books: five years for 5 g of crystal meth, the crack of the '90s. Mandatory minimums remain political beasts, and it would probably take Nixon-goes-to-China leadership from a Republican to turn public opinion against them. Either that or more Jean Valjeans serving 10-year sentences for stealing steaks.

"All other things being equal, the removal of known criminals from society ipso facto will reduce the crime rate."

IMPRISONING CRIMINALS PREVENTS CRIME

Andrew Peyton Thomas

Imprisoning criminals reduces the crime rate because it removes criminals from society, thus limiting their ability to commit more crimes, argues Andrew Peyton Thomas in the following viewpoint. In addition, imprisoning criminals teaches them that they will be punished for their crime, Thomas maintains, which acts as a strong deterrent in the future. As long as society continues to incarcerate criminals, Thomas contends that the crime rate will continue to fall. Thomas is an attorney and author of *Crime and the Sacking of America: The Roots of Chaos*.

As you read, consider the following questions:

1. What are the two ways in which incarceration can reduce the crime rate, according to the author?
2. In the author's opinion, why are violent crimes such as murder and rape not as well suited to the imprisonment-reduces-crime theory?
3. Which group of criminals has the highest recidivism rate, according to Thomas?

Reprinted from Andrew Peyton Thomas, "More Time, Less Crime," *The Weekly Standard*, November 30–December 7, 1998, with the permission of *The Weekly Standard*. Copyright, News America Inc.

F ox Butterfield of the *New York Times* regularly reports on what he sees as one of the great anomalies of the age: Incarceration rates are rising while crime rates are falling. An August 1998 article titled "Prison Population Growing Although Crime Rate Drops" was typical. Butterfield began, "The nation's prison population grew by 5.2 percent in 1997, according to the Justice Department, even though crime has been declining for six straight years, suggesting that the imprisonment boom has developed a built-in growth dynamic independent of the crime rate, experts say."

By "experts say," Butterfield meant that many liberal criminologists agree with him. To him and his likeminded profs, the continued rise in incarceration rates during a time of declining crime rates is a mystery tinged with injustice. As Butterfield stated in a January 1998 article, the rise in incarceration rates is prompting "troublesome questions" about "whether the United States is relying too heavily on prison sentences to combat drugs and whether the prison boom has become self-perpetuating."

Yet Butterfield's own article in August had an answer to these questions. He noted that 52 percent of the total increase in male prisoners in 1997 came from criminals convicted of violent offenses. Only anarchists would pronounce this a tragedy.

As for drug offenses, the vast majority of inmates are career criminals, as demonstrated in Arizona, where in 1996 voters approved a drug-liberalization ballot initiative. The initiative would have required the release of all inmates sentenced for first-time drug offenses—about 1,000 inmates in all. But in 1997, the state legislature amended the law to disqualify from this amnesty all first-time drug inmates previously convicted of a felony. As a result, the number of inmates entitled to freedom shrank to 53. Americans clearly are locking up the right people.

Common sense and empirical knowledge conspire against the thesis that crime rates and incarceration rates are unrelated. After all, the simplest explanation for today's declining crime rates is the simultaneous rise in incarceration rates. In other words, all other things being equal, the removal of known criminals from society *ipso facto* will reduce the crime rate.

TESTING THE THEORY

How do we test this? First, we look for data on crime rates and incarceration rates. In 1980, America began an unprecedented boom in prison construction. This new space has not gone empty: From 1980 to 1996, the incarceration rate lurched upward 209 percent. Over the same 16 years, there has been a relatively steady decrease in the serious-crime rate—a decrease of 31 percent.

In the 1990s, as word spread on the street that serious crimes would provoke serious punishment, crime rates fell dramatically. From 1991 to 1996, incarceration rates rose 38 percent. The serious-crime rate during the same period fell 22 percent. As more violent offenders—murderers, rapists, and the like—were taken out of circulation, the violent-crime rate similarly declined 16 percent.

INCARCERATION'S EFFECT

Next we should consider the effect of incarceration on specific crimes. Prison can reduce the crime rate in two ways: (a) by teaching criminals that they will suffer punishment for breaking the law (which deters people from committing crimes), and (b) by removing criminals from society (which incapacitates them). As a result, we would expect to see the strongest relationship between crime rates and incarceration rates for those offenses for which both deterrence and incapacitation are operative.

Except for robberies, violent crimes are not well suited to this type of analysis. Most murders, rapes, and other violent crimes are not committed in a serial fashion. Also, most violent criminals have relatively low recidivism rates. Tough incarceration rates may deter these criminals, but because violent criminals, by and large, do not commit many crimes of the same type, locking them up offers little marginal return in the way of incapacitation.

BURGLARY

The most appropriate crime for testing both the deterrence effects and the incapacitation effects of incarceration is burglary. Burglars have the highest recidivism rate of all serious offenders. Nationwide, the recidivism rate for burglary is just under 50 percent. This is higher than even the recidivism rate for drug offenders. If not for incarceration, a very high percentage of burglars would simply keep on burglarizing

The data suggest a strong connection between burglary rates and incarceration rates. When the prison-building boom began in 1980, the burglary rate started to descend. Except for the mid-1980s, when the number of drug-related crimes rose, the decline in burglary rates has been steady. The burglary rate dropped 44 percent from 1980 to 1996. In the 1990s, the burglary rate fell 25 percent in just six years. This was, again, during the same period in which the overall incarceration rate rose 38 percent. Deterrence and incapacitation combined to produce an impressive decline in burglary rates.

The same analysis holds true for robbery rates. Like burglary, robbery—the taking of property from another by force or threat thereof—is a crime typically committed in serial fashion. Robbers, like burglars, have high recidivism rates—the highest recidivism rates of any violent offenders. From 1991 to 1996, robbery rates fell 26 percent (almost identical to the 25 percent decline in the burglary rate). Burglaries and robberies have declined at a faster rate in the 1990s than any other serious crimes.

THE GREAT MYSTERY IS SOLVED

Why is there so much less crime? The *New York Times* stumbled onto the truth while providing a shining example of the liberal establishment's lack of common sense. Here's the headline from September 28, 1997: CRIME KEEPS ON FALLING, BUT PRISONS KEEP ON FILLING. Did they say "but"? Shouldn't it be "*As* PRISONS KEEP ON FILLING"? The story, by Fox Butterfield, begins by noting the decline in crime, then asks: "So why is the number of inmates in prisons and jails around the nation still going up? Last year, it reached almost 1.7 million, up about seven percent a year since 1990."

Now, ordinary people might think there's actually a *connection* between throwing criminals in the slammer and crime going down, but to the enlightened ones who choose which news is fit to print, it remains one of the Great Mysteries.

The fact is that of course prisons reduce crime.

Rush Limbaugh, *The Limbaugh Letter*, February 1998.

We have seen in this decade that when career criminals are sent to prison, crime rates drop. Of course, improved police work, greater community involvement, teenage curfews, and other reforms have reinforced these trends. And the success enjoyed to date scarcely guarantees future success. Even if the violent-crime rate continued to decline at its current rate, it would take 25 years for America to return to the violent-crime rate it enjoyed in 1960. This is highly unlikely for many reasons, including the cyclical nature of crime rates, the demographic bulge of young men coming of age over the next decade, and the fact that incarceration rates today are still quite low, relative to where they were in the late 1950s.

SOCIETY MEANS BUSINESS

Still, those of us who, until recently, thought that crime rates would continue to rise because of social dissolution should admit that we underestimated the effectiveness of simple punishment. Americans may cherish many of the wrong values today, but at least we love our lives and property enough to be willing to lock up large numbers of criminals in expensive, out-of-the-way places. Criminals, as a result, are learning that society means business. As long as we drive this lesson home—and as long as America as a whole is spared the pathologies most acutely associated with the inner city—permanent reductions in our crime rates will be a realistic goal.

"Much more [than incarcerating offenders] is reducing crime, though: Added police. . . . Measures reducing the flow of guns onto the streets. A decrease in the cocaine trade. Good economic times."

IMPRISONING CRIMINALS IS ONLY ONE OF MANY FACTORS THAT PREVENT CRIME

Neal R. Peirce

As part of the war on drugs that began in the 1970s, many states began requiring drug abusers to serve harsh, mandatory prison terms. Neal R. Peirce argues in the following viewpoint that the continued incarceration of nonviolent drug abusers—a group that makes up the majority of prisoners—has little effect on the crime rate. According to Peirce, the crime rate is dropping because of better policing, strict gun control laws, and a good economy that provides alternatives to crime. In addition, funding drug treatment and other crime prevention programs would reduce the crime rate even further. Peirce is a syndicated columnist.

As you read, consider the following questions:

1. How does the U.S. incarceration rate compare to that of other countries, according to the author?
2. What is the "prison-industrial complex," according to Eric Schlosser, as cited by Peirce?
3. In Peirce's view, why is celebrating the declining crime rate reprehensible?

Reprinted from Neal R. Peirce, "The Prison Craze and the Crime Rate," syndicated column, January 5, 1999, with permission. Copyright ©1999 Washington Post Writers Group.

The violent crime rate in America continues to plummet. It's off 21 percent since 1993, 7 percent in 1997 alone. Murders in the country's 10 largest cities declined 12 percent in 1998. Our streets are certifiably the safest they've been since the 1970s.

But there's grim news, too, summarized by writer Eric Schlosser in a disturbing report—"The Prison-Industrial Complex"—in *The Atlantic Monthly*.

THE WORLD'S HIGHEST INCARCERATION RATE

Some 1.8 million Americans are behind bars, in federal and state prisons and local jails. We are imprisoning more people than any other nation on Earth, even Communist China. We've achieved the highest incarceration rate in human history for nonpolitical offenses.

Among our prisoners are dangerous folks we all want to see locked up—roughly 150,000 armed robbers, 125,000 murderers, 100,000 sex offenders. But of the people now going to prison, Schlosser reports, less than a third have committed a violent crime. Drug-related cases predominate:

"Crimes that in other countries would usually lead to community service, fines or drug treatment—or not be considered crimes at all—in the United States now lead to a prison term, by far the most expensive form of punishment."

The United States actually had a rather steady 20th-century rate of imprisonment—about 110 inmates for every 100,000 people—until the 1970s. Then New York's Gov. Nelson Rockefeller suddenly suggested every illegal drug dealer be punished with a mandatory prison sentence of life without parole.

Across the country, politicians of both parties emulated Rockefeller, pushing multiple types of mandatory sentencing laws. As battalions of drug offenders got caught, our governments constructed some 1,000 new prisons in 20 years. Virtually all are now filled to the gills, many dangerously overcrowded. California alone now has more inmates than France, Great Britain, Germany, Japan, Singapore and the Netherlands combined. Our national incarceration rate is 445 per 100,000.

And things may still get worse. Sentencing laws and parole policies in Georgia, for example, are so stiff that the governor's budget office recently predicted Georgia prisons would double in size in a decade. Likely cost: over $4 billion.

THE PRISON BOOM

We've created a self-perpetuating prison boom, what Schlosser labels a "prison-industrial complex" as potent as the "military-industrial complex" President Dwight D. Eisenhower warned of.

The active partners in this new complex are politicians using fear of crime to garner votes, low-income rural areas clawing for new prisons as a cornerstone of economic development, private companies angling to share in the lucrative $35-billion-a-year prison industry, and government officials expanding their bureaucratic empires.

So now we must ask: Has the prison boom swept up so many criminals it's responsible for dropping crime rates?

The answer: in part, of course. Incarcerated offenders are safely (albeit temporarily) off the streets.

Not Necessarily a Cause-and-Effect Relationship

It is difficult to test theories about the impact of imprisonment on crime rates. Just because two facts exist does not necessarily mean there is a cause and effect relationship between them. For example, few people would agree that if crime rates rose when the imprisonment rate rose that the increase in imprisonment *caused* the increase in crime. One immediately asks what else was going on that might influence these trends.

The relationship between imprisonment and crime is very difficult to ascertain, in part because it is difficult to isolate these factors from other social and economic variables which probably influence the level of crime, such as demographic shifts, unemployment rates, divorce rates, and education levels.

Campaign for an Effective Crime Policy's briefing paper "What Every Policymaker Should Know About Imprisonment and the Crime Rate," February 1995.

Much more is reducing crime, though: Added police, linked with an historic rise in community policing and computer-based crime tracking and dispatch. The Brady bill and other measures reducing the flow of guns onto the streets. A decrease in the cocaine trade. Good economic times providing alternatives to crime.

Drug Treatment Programs

So could we reduce crime without our obscene prison building binge? Certainly. Prisons have become a revolving door for poor, highly dysfunctional, often illiterate drug abusers. Our governments are generally too chintzy to offer them drug treatment, behind bars or on the street.

Diverting some of the billions now going to the prison-industrial complex for drug treatment and other prevention efforts could start us on a much saner course.

RACE

Another gnawing issue is race. Black men are five times as likely to be arrested for drug offenses as whites (even though whites and blacks have similar abuse levels). The incarceration rate for black males was 3,096 per 100,000 in 1996, eight times the rate for white men (370 per 100,000) and more than double the rate for Hispanic men.

Roughly half our inmates are African-American. One of every 14 black men is now in prison; one of four is imprisoned at some point. The new prisons they get sent to are overwhelmingly in white, rural areas, and their guards rural whites.

So any idea of celebrating our declining crime rates because of high incarceration rates is reprehensible on three counts: the bestial nature of prison life; a race-based denial of equal rights and civil rights reminiscent of the old South Africa; and a bloated, overwhelmingly white prison-industrial complex making money off the whole.

The prison craze besmirches the name of America. In the best of economic times, in a nation dominant on the world stage, it's more intolerable than ever. In community-based policing and neighborhood-oriented prevention programs, we've begun to build a better way. Now we need a vigorous political debate: How to build safer communities without incarcerating so many millions of our fellow citizens.

"The police should be vigilant about the minor, 'quality of life' infractions that heighten discomfort and fear. By doing that, . . . inroads would be made against the people who were committing more serious crimes."

A STRONG POLICE PRESENCE PREVENTS CRIME

Allan C. Brownfeld

In the following viewpoint, Allan C. Brownfeld argues that the astronomical drop in New York City's crime rate can be traced to the police's "zero tolerance" policy for relatively minor infractions such as jumping turnstiles at subway stations and public drinking, and to having police walk a beat instead of responding to calls in cars. Some people who were arrested on such minor charges were found to be armed, and Brownfeld contends that by following through on the zero tolerance policy, the police reduced the likelihood that these offenders would commit more serious crimes in the future. Brownfeld is a contributing editor to the *St. Croix Review*, a bimonthly publication of the conservative organization Religion and Society, Inc.

As you read, consider the following questions:
1. What are the root causes of crime, according to liberals and conservatives as cited by James Traub?
2. What is the "broken windows theory," as described by James Q. Wilson?
3. What is the best defense of punishment, according to John J. DiIulio Jr.?

Reprinted from Allan C. Brownfeld, "Important Lessons to Be Learned from New York's War on Crime," Ramblings, *St. Croix Review*, April 1997, with permission.

In 1996, New York City had 983 murders. The last time New York had fewer than one thousand murders was 1968. Only four years ago, in 1992, two thousand people were murdered in the city. Robberies are down by thirty-one per cent. In fact, the drop in New York's crime rate over the last few years has been so dramatic that it has accounted for fully one-third of the total national reduction of crime.

These figures represent a clear victory for the policing philosophy that Mayor Rudolph Giuliani and his former police commissioner, William Bratton, introduced in 1994. Writing in *The New Republic*, James Traub notes that the success of New York's crime fighting effort:

> calls into question a central assumption of both the liberal and conservative approach to crime—the idea that the only way to make a serious reduction in crime is to address its root causes. Liberals and conservatives have shared this view for years, disagreeing only on the question of what the root cause is. For liberals, crime results from the despair induced by poverty, unemployment, and poor schooling. Conservatives blame "moral poverty"—the effect on the underclass of the collapse of the moral guidance that once came from families, churches, and the larger culture.

PROTECTING THE QUALITY OF LIFE

Mayor Giuliani and Commissioner Bratton made New York's quality of life the starting point in their enforcement approach. Men drinking beer in front of a bodega, for example, were issued a summons that could lead to a court appearance and a fine. "Pretty soon," police officer Odanel Irias told Traub, who accompanied him on his rounds in the Washington Heights neighborhood,

> There's nobody urinating in the streets, because nobody's drinking beer. You don't get so much loud noise and disruption. You take care of the little things and the big things take care of themselves. Say you have four guys drinking in the street. All of a sudden, here comes a fight, here comes a knife, here comes a gun, here comes a body. But if they know you're going to be around, they watch themselves.

Policemen were put back to walking the beat—not responding in squad cars when trouble had already occurred. Officers were authorized to pat down anyone to whom they had issued a summons, even for a minor infraction. The focus on weapons helped to reduce the murder rate sharply. "Once you start leaving your gun at home, you're less likely to kill someone in a fight," Irias said.

What New York officials did was broaden the focus of law enforcement, making the police presence clear in the community. In addition to solving a problem which has already taken place, New York moved toward disrupting street crime, and specifically the drug trade. Andrew Linares, the owner of a shop in Washington Heights, stated that,

> Double or triple parking used to be a common thing two or three years ago; now it's not. It sounds goofy, but it does give you a gauge of control, that there is authority, there is order. You don't see the mobs on the street.

THE BROKEN WINDOWS THEORY

In the book *Fixing Broken Windows* by George Kelling, who was a key adviser to Police Commissioner Bratton, and Catherine Coles, a lawyer and anthropologist who studies cities, it is pointed out that the job of public authorities is not only to apprehend criminals but to give citizens confidence that order is being maintained in their neighborhoods. In the introduction, Professor James Q. Wilson, an authority on criminal justice, writes that,

> If a factory or office window is broken, passersby observing it will conclude that no one cares or no one is in charge. In time, a few will begin throwing rocks to break more windows. Soon all the windows will be broken, and now passersby will think that not only is no one in charge of the building, no one is in charge of the street on which it faces. . . . Small disorders lead to larger and larger ones, and perhaps even to crime.

Under Bratton, the issue of "quality of life" became paramount. No drinking on the streets would be permitted, for example. Earlier, as chief of the Transit Police, Bratton began arresting fare jumpers and learned something which was unexpected: many of them were armed. By arresting them for jumping the subway turnstile, they were apprehended before they committed an armed robbery—or worse.

FIGHTING CRIME VERSUS RESPONDING TO CRIME

In an article, "The Crime Buster," about one of Commissioner Bratton's chief lieutenants, James Maple, *New Yorker* correspondent David Remnick writes that

> By the time Maple made lieutenant in Transit, he had also made a name for himself by running decoy squads in the subway. The squads arrested hundreds of teenage muggers who worked in gangs—a phenomenon known, in the mid-1980s, as wolf-packs. So successful were the decoys (cops posing, generically, as "the

Jewish lawyer," "the blind man," "the casual couple") that even the national media took notice. . . . Jack told anyone who would listen that until the entire police force got out of its rut—until officers got out of their patrol cars and started fighting crime instead of responding to 911 calls—until that happened, the crime rate would keep climbing. . . . Why stop with the subways? Why not raid the crack houses every day until they were shut down!

The ideas of policing being implemented in New York are hardly new, although they have been largely ignored. In a 1982 article in the *The Atlantic Monthly*, James Q. Wilson and George Kelling argued that society had undergone a serious decline in standards of behavior, that we had learned to tolerate a range of once forbidden conditions. In New York City, public drinking and urination, mild harassment and farebeating, had become acceptable. In Wilson and Kellings' view, the police should be vigilant about the minor, "quality of life" infractions that heighten discomfort and fear. By doing that, they believed, inroads would be made against the people who were committing more serious crimes. Finally, these ideas have been implemented in New York to great success.

THE LIBERAL VIEW OF PUNISHMENT

Criminologist Charles H. Logan of the University of Connecticut and political scientist John J. DiIulio, Jr. of Princeton point out that the root of the liberal misunderstanding of how to approach crime and criminals is their view that, somehow, punishing of wrong-doers is bad:

It is largely because they are opposed to punishment generally and to imprisonment in particular that many people argue too strongly that we must address the root causes of crime, that our criminal justice system discriminates, that we are overly punitive . . . that prisons are too costly and overcrowded. . . . The "Big Myth" is that punishment has no value in itself; that it is intrinsically evil and can be justified as a necessary evil only if it can be shown to have some overriding value, such as social order. . . . The best defense of punishment is not that it upholds the social order, but that it fosters important moral and cultural values. Legal punishment is a legitimate and, if properly defined and administered, even a noble aspect of our culture. Imprisonment, in order to be respectable, does not need to be defined as "corrections," or as "treatment," or as "education," or as "protection of society.". . . Principles and fair punishment for wrongdoing treats individuals as persons and as human beings, rather than as objects. Punishment is an affirmation of the autonomous responsibility and dignity of the individual.

The endless discussion of "root causes" of crime rather than of the best means to control it is, argues economist Thomas Sowell in his book *The Vision of the Anointed*, an example of how so many intellectuals, in particular, misunderstand human nature. He declares that many

are especially reluctant to see human nature as the source of the evils they wish to eradicate. Instead, they seek *special* causes of particular evils. Nothing so exemplifies this approach as the perennial attempts to get at the "root causes," as it is phrased, of crime. There seems to be no awareness that people commit crimes because they are human beings. That is, people's natural impulses are to favor themselves over others and to disregard the harm they create in trying to satisfy their own desires the easiest way. If most people do not behave this way with complete shamelessness in most things, it is because they have been through a long process of becoming civilized—and because this process is buttressed by law enforcement. Civilization has been aptly called a "thin crust over a volcano." The anointed (liberal intellectuals) are constantly picking at that crust.

Now, New York City has attempted to restore that "thin crust" of civilization by punishing wrongdoing, putting policemen back on the streets where they belong, and preventing crime before it occurs. The rest of the nation would do well to study New York's policies and emulate its example.

> "Most of the decline [in the crime rate] that has occurred would have occurred' without more police on the streets."

A STRONG POLICE PRESENCE DOES NOT PREVENT CRIME

Anthony Arnove

An aging population and the decline in the use of crack cocaine are more responsible for the drop in crime rates than a strong police presence, argues Anthony Arnove in the following viewpoint. In fact, Arnove contends, putting more police on the street and giving them the power and authority to enforce "zero tolerance" policies may actually increase police violence and corruption because the officers believe they are above the law. Arnove is a writer for *Socialist Worker*, a publication of the National Socialist Party.

As you read, consider the following questions:

1. How have crime rates changed since the mid-1970s, according to the author?
2. What four reasons does the author give for the drop in crime rates?
3. By what percentage did police brutality complaints increase in New York City in the first half of 1995, as cited by Arnove?

Reprinted from Anthony Arnove, "Will More Cops Stop Crime?" *Socialist Worker*, March 15, 1996, with permission.

For years, politicians have manipulated people's fear of "sky-rocketing" crime in the U.S.

Republicans and Democrats alike increasingly advocate "get tough on crime" policies, calling for harsher mandatory prison sentences and more cops on the streets. . . .

Yet at the same time as the news media and politicians suggest that crime rates are soaring, FBI statistics actually show a decline in violent crime since 1992.

The statistics show a 3 percent overall drop in serious crimes in 1994, a 2 percent decline in 1993, and a 3 percent decrease in 1992.

Violent crimes reported to the FBI fell by 4 percent in 1994.

[The reason] why crime is down in many cities . . . has little to do with more cops on the streets or the "get-tough" talk of the politicians.

On the contrary, there has been a sharp increase in police corruption and violence, because cops feel they are free to do as they please.

LITTLE CHANGE

The most significant decline in crime rates has come in cities with over 1 million people, which saw a 6 percent decrease in reported violent crime in 1995.

Now, politicians are fighting for the credit. Tough prison sentences and aggressive policing are beginning to pay off, they claim.

But has putting more police on the streets really brought down crime?

Despite all the hysteria and intensified media coverage, violent crime levels in the U.S. are about the same as they were in the early 1970s—though crime rates rose and fell during the late 1970s and the 1980s.

According to George Washington University sociologist William Chambliss, "The best available data . . . show that the crime rate has not changed significantly in the last 20 years."

Looking at longer trends, national crime rates, especially murder rates, have not dropped significantly from 1993 to 1996.

The period of 1980 to 1985 actually saw a sharper decline in the national murder rate—only to see it climb from 1986 to 1991.

In fact, national crime rates have periodically gone through short cycles that do not necessarily reflect long-term trends.

"The figures wiggle from year to year, like the stock market," explains Harold Snyder, a researcher at the National Center for Juvenile Justice in Pittsburgh.

But media coverage of crime has soared, as politicians and the media manipulate working people's fears.

Their aim is to blame crime for social problems such as lousy schools, decaying neighborhoods and declining standards of living for most Americans—and to turn attention away from the real causes of these problems.

As *New York Times* economic analyst Louis Uchitelle wrote in an article on corporate layoffs on March 3, 1996, "Roughly 50 percent more people, about 3 million, are affected by layoffs each year than the 2 million victims of violent crimes."

But politicians make careers out of calling for more cops while covering for the corporations that make billions in profits and millions for their CEOs as they throw more and more workers out of work.

THE REAL REASONS BEHIND THE DROP IN CRIME RATES

The most compelling explanations for a drop in crime in recent years point to reasons other than more police.

Instead, people who study crime point to:

• The aging population in the U.S., which tends to bring down crime rates;

• The decline in the use of crack cocaine, which was related to an increase in drug-related violent crimes in the late 1980s;

• An increase in gang truces and changes in drug turf war battles; and

• A shift in some crime from large cities to suburban and rural areas.

According to James Alan Fox, a criminologist at Northeastern University, "Most of the decline that has occurred would have occurred" without more police on the streets.

"The baby boom generation, which comprises almost a third of the population, is getting older" and committing fewer crimes, Fox said.

Another trend that has nothing to do with cops is the decline of crack cocaine use, as more people have become aware of the effects of crack and as the use of heroin increases.

In addition, a number of drug turf wars and inter-gang rivalries have settled in recent years in cities such as New York and Los Angeles, bringing down the number of gang-related deaths.

In many cases, these settlements were inspired by the gang truce signed in the aftermath of the Los Angeles uprising against racism and police brutality after the Rodney King verdict was announced. [Four white Los Angeles police officers were acquitted in 1992 of police brutality charges in the beating of black motorist Rodney King in March 1991.]

New York City's Washington Heights neighborhood saw a decline in gang-related deaths from 119 people in 1991 to 56 in 1994 because of new understandings between dealers about areas they controlled.

GANG-RELATED CRIME

Meanwhile, Queens has seen drops in gang-related crime because of changes in Latin American drug battles in Colombia, controlled by the Cali cartel, which has "forced drug networks to become more efficient and less violent," according to the *New York Times*.

Local prosecutors and federal officials who monitor the Colombian drug trade told the *Times* that the reasons for the decline in crime in Queens "have less to do with the police and more to do with the [Cali] cartel itself."

"These officials say the cartel has reorganized, tamping down the internal battles that arose after the Colombian police arrested six cartel kingpins" in 1995.

POVERTY

All of these changes have helped to bring down crime rates in urban areas, but another factor in declining crime rates in cities is people moving—as poverty forces some people away from cities looking for employment and housing, all too often finding unemployment and discrimination or poverty-level wages instead.

Poverty, especially childhood poverty, has been growing faster in rural and in suburban areas than in major cities since 1980.

Poverty and acts of passion are at the roots of most crimes—something that cops can do nothing about.

In fact, the real role of cops is to preserve an unequal and violent society.

People who study crime have suggested a number of reasons why crime is down in New York City and around the country.

But New York City Police Commissioner William Bratton has become a "poster boy" for the claim that tougher "community policing" has brought down crime—and that more cops will bring down crime even further.

In contrast to newspaper images of friendly cops playing basketball with Black teenagers, Bratton's strategy for "community policing" has given New York cops the freedom to make more aggressive arrests and to violate civil liberties freely.

"Much of the new aggressiveness from street cops . . . stems from the tough-talking rhetoric at the top," New York *Newsday* reported in April 1995.

"High-ranking law-enforcement officials say privately that . . . the [police] department's top brass have sent a subtle message to cops that there is a new no-holds-barred approach to fighting crime."

ASSERTIVE POLICING LEADS TO MORE CONFRONTATIONS

"Assertive policing," an aggressive variant of what's often called community policing, has been credited with sharply reducing crime throughout New York City. It is being copied in Washington, Houston, St. Louis and other cities.

Mayor Rudy Giuliani has dubbed his city's version zero tolerance," because it means enforcing every law, no matter how minor, from jaywalking to playing loud music. . . .

The 70th Precinct has embraced assertive policing. The cops have gotten out of their patrol cars and started walking the streets. The precinct's force has increased from 210 to 330 since 1991. Now, if you're drinking beer on the sidewalk, you're going to pour it out. If you're playing your boombox too loud, you're going to turn it down. And some residents say assertive policing means that if you talk back to a cop here, you're going to get busted, perhaps even beaten.

Dennis Cauchon, *USA Today*, August 27, 1997.

Bratton has ordered cops to arrest people for any possible violation—from scrawling graffiti to public drinking—as part of a "proactive" policing strategy.

As the *New York Times* reported, "In the crackdown on minor offenses, like public beer drinking, urination and unlicensed street vending, Mr. Bratton's department found new ways to frisk people for guns and check their records for outstanding warrants.

"Suddenly, people brought into precinct station houses for nothing more serious than graffiti scrawling were pressed for information about drug or gun dealing."

PETTY MISDEMEANORS

Arrests in New York City climbed by more than 25 percent in 1995, mostly for petty misdemeanors.

According to Norman Siegel, executive director of the New York Civil Liberties Union, "The police are aggressive and potentially hostile towards citizens who are not engaged in any illegal or criminal activities."

Given Bratton's strategy, it is not surprising that complaints about police brutality in New York have soared.

According to the Civilian Complaint Review Board (CCRB), complaints rose 31.8 percent in the first half of 1995.

"Complaints against New York cops charging brutality, racism and other offenses have gone through the roof since tough-talking Police Commissioner Bratton took control [in 1994]," the conservative *New York Post* wrote after studying the CCRB's figures.

The CCRB found that allegations of excessive force were up 26.3 percent, and abuse of authority went up 40.3 percent in 1995. The increase follows a 37 percent rise in 1994.

Bratton's "no-holds-barred" policing has clearly targeted poor Black and Latino youth. CCRB figures show that 49 percent of people filing police brutality rates were Black and 24.6 percent were Hispanic.

"THE BRATTON WAY"

When New York cop Francis Livoti killed 23-year-old Anthony Baez, in police custody in December 1994 after Baez threw a football that accidentally hit his police cruiser, one of his commanding sergeants bragged to the *New York Times* that Livoti "polices the Bratton way, aggressively and proactively."

One month after Baez was murdered, another New York cop explained to the *New York Post* what "policing the Bratton way" really means: "Bratton wants us to break heads—we'll break heads."

In July, when he was confronted by 75 activists from Parents Against Police Brutality—including Margarita Rosario, whose 18-year-old son Anthony was shot 14 times in the back by two cops as he laid on his stomach—Bratton told protesters that they were "making fools" of themselves and said, "No one is listening to you."

"Bratton went ballistic," the *New York Daily News* reported.

In April 1994, three officers killed Ernest Savon, a Black 22-year-old from Staten Island who was in their custody, by choking him to death.

When confronted, Bratton told reporters, "I don't think it has as much to do with police assertiveness or aggressiveness as just that we now have a society where it's become the norm to resist arrest."

This is a complete lie, but it sends a clear signal to the 38,500 officers in New York that they can brutalize and murder with almost total impunity and claim later that their victim—no matter what the evidence—was "resisting arrest."

PERIODICAL BIBLIOGRAPHY

The following articles have been selected to supplement the diverse views presented in this chapter. Addresses are provided for periodicals not indexed in the *Readers' Guide to Periodical Literature*, the *Alternative Press Index*, the *Social Sciences Index*, or the *Index to Legal Periodicals and Books*.

Walter Berns	"Crime in the Public Mind," *Society*, March/April 1997.
Barry Lee Coyne	"For Those Who Cringe at Crime," *Christian Social Action*, December 1997. Available from 100 Maryland Ave. NE, Washington, DC 20002.
John J. DiIulio Jr.	"Arresting Ideas," *Policy Review*, Fall 1995.
Craig Donegan	"Preventing Juvenile Crime," *CQ Researcher*, March 15, 1996. Available from 1414 22nd St. NW, Washington, DC 20037.
David R. Francis	"Just Proven: Prisons Do Keep Down Crime," *Christian Science Monitor*, January 19, 1996.
Bob Herbert	"The Keys to Cutting Crime," *Liberal Opinion*, October 13, 1997. Available from PO Box 880, Vinton, IA 52349-0880.
Shari Huffman	"Taking Back Their Neighborhoods," *Christian Social Action*, May 1997.
Mike Males and Faye Docuyanan	"Crackdown on Kids," *Progressive*, February 1996.
Edmund F. McGarrell	"Cutting Crime Through Police-Citizen Cooperation," *Outlook*, Spring 1998. Available from 5395 Emerson Way, Indianapolis, IN 46226.
Eugene H. Methvin	"Mugged by Reality," *Policy Review*, July/August 1997.
George E. Pataki	"Death Penalty *Is* a Deterrent," *USA Today*, March 1997.
Charley Reese	"Crime Problem Has Simple Solution," *Conservative Chronicle*, December 9, 1998. Available from PO Box 37077, Boone, IA 50037-0077.
Robert Warburton	"'Lock 'Em Up and Leave 'Em There!'" *Christian Social Action*, October 1997.
Robert L. Woodson	"Reclaiming the Lives of Young People," *USA Today*, September 1997.

For Further Discussion

Chapter 1

1. Richard J. Herrnstein and Douglas S. Massey's definition of crime differs from that of Jeff Milder and the John Howard Society of Alberta. How does an author's definition of crime affect his argument about what causes crime?

2. Dave Grossman argues that media violence desensitizes children to the horror and pain of violence, therefore making it easier for them to kill. John Katz contends, however, that it is not violence in the media that influences children to kill, but the easy availability of guns. Which argument is stronger? Support your answer with examples from the viewpoints.

Chapter 2

1. Bill Kolender is a county sheriff who believes that a concealed weapon would be useless as a means of protection against a criminal. John R. Lott Jr. is a researcher who contends that crime decreases when criminals think their potential victims may be carrying concealed weapons. In your opinion, could carrying a concealed weapon reduce crime and yet still be worthless as protection against crime? Why or why not? Support your answer.

2. Handgun Control, Inc. and Tanya K. Metaksa debate the pros and cons of a waiting period versus an instant background check for purchasing handguns. List the advantages and disadvantages of each system. In your opinion, which is the better program for detecting unlawful buyers? Support your answer. Should the purpose of delaying homicidal or suicidal people from taking possession of a handgun be considered when determining a program's effectiveness in deterring crime? Why or why not?

Chapter 3

1. Don Boys argues that juvenile rapists and murderers should be given the same punishment as adult criminals, including the death penalty. Based on your reading of the viewpoints, do you think that violent juvenile criminals should receive adult sentences? Explain your answer.

2. According to Roger Conner, cities should be allowed to infringe upon the rights of individuals in order to protect the good of society. In your opinion, is this an equal trade? Why or why not? Which circumstances, if any, would justify limiting or suspending the rights of individuals in order to protect

the common good?

3. John Leo argues that parental responsibility laws could be the wake-up call some parents need to properly supervise their children. Mary Ann Perga contends that parental responsibility laws would have little effect on changing teen behavior. Do you think parents should be held accountable for their children's criminal actions? Should the seriousness of the crime be a factor? Are your answers the same if the children lie or sneak out without their parents' knowledge? Explain your answers.

4. Geoffrey Canada argues that parents should be the ones to set curfews for teens. Do you believe that curfews set by the government unduly infringe upon the rights of teens? Or are they justified as a means of keeping society and other teens safe from the threat of teen violence, as the *San Diego Union-Tribune* argues? Defend your answer with examples from the viewpoints.

CHAPTER 4

1. Jay Johansen and Eric M. Freedman use national and state statistics to support their views of the death penalty's deterrence effect on murder rates. What effect, if any, does the fact that Texas executes more death row prisoners than all the other states combined have on these statistics? In your opinion, does the death penalty deter violent crime? Why or why not?

2. Dan Lungren argues that the criminals who are imprisoned under the "three strikes" law are violent felons who get what they deserve. According to John Cloud, however, many of those imprisoned by the "three strikes" law are nonviolent drug users who pose no threat to society. Based on your reading of the viewpoints, should the "three strikes" law remain as it is or should it be amended or repealed? Explain your answer.

3. Andrew Peyton Thomas argues that naturally the crime rate will fall as criminals are imprisoned for their crimes. Neal R. Peirce contends that other factors are also responsible for the falling crime rate. Which argument is stronger? Could both arguments be correct? Support your answer with examples from the viewpoints.

Organizations to Contact

The editors have compiled the following list of organizations concerned with the issues debated in this book. The descriptions are derived from materials provided by the organizations. All have publications or information available for interested readers. The list was compiled on the date of publication of the present volume; the information provided here may change. Be aware that many organizations take several weeks or longer to respond to inquiries, so allow as much time as possible.

American Civil Liberties Union (ACLU)
125 Broad St., 18th Fl., New York, NY 10004-2400
(212) 549-2500
e-mail: aclu@aclu.org • website: http://www.aclu.org
The ACLU is a national organization that works to defend Americans' civil rights as guaranteed by the U.S. Constitution. It opposes curfew laws for juveniles and others and seeks to protect the public-assembly rights of gang members or people associated with gangs. Among the ACLU's numerous publications are the handbook *The Rights of Prisoners: A Comprehensive Guide to the Legal Rights of Prisoners Under Current Law*, and the briefing paper "Crime and Civil Liberties."

Campaign for an Effective Crime Policy
918 F St. NW, Suite 505, Washington, DC 20004
(202) 628-1903 • fax: (202) 628-1091
e-mail: staff@crimepolicy.org • website: http://www.crimepolicy.org
Launched in 1992 by a group of criminal justice leaders, the nonpartisan Campaign for an Effective Crime Policy advocates alternative sentencing policies. It also works to educate the public about the relative effectiveness of various strategies for improving public safety. The Campaign has published a series of reports on issues in criminal justice, including "'Three Strikes' Laws: Five Years Later."

Cato Institute
1000 Massachusetts Ave. NW, Washington, DC 20001-5403
(202) 842-0200 • fax: (202) 842-3490
e-mail: cato@cato.org • website: http://www.cato.org
The institute is a libertarian public policy research foundation dedicated to limiting the role of government and protecting individual liberties. It opposes gun control measures and the death penalty and supports concealed-carry laws. The institute evaluates government policies and offers reform proposals in its publication *Policy Analysis*. Topics include "Crime, Police, and Root Causes" and "Prison Blues: How America's Foolish Sentencing Policies Endanger Public Safety." In addition, the institute publishes the quarterly magazine *Regulation*, the bimonthly *Cato Policy Report*, and numerous books.

Coalition to Stop Gun Violence (CSGV)
1000 16th St. NW, Suite 603, Washington, DC 20036-5705
(202) 530-0340
e-mail: noguns@aol.com • website: http://www.gunfree.org

Formerly the National Coalition to Ban Handguns, the coalition lobbies at the local, state, and federal levels to ban the sale of handguns and assault weapons to individuals. It also litigates cases against firearms makers. Its publications include various informational sheets on gun violence and the *Stop Gun Violence Newsletter* and the *Firearms Litigation Reporter*.

Families Against Mandatory Minimums (FAMM)
1612 K St. NW, Suite 1400, Washington, DC 20006
(202) 822-6700 • fax: (202) 822-6704
e-mail: famm@famm.org • website: http://www.famm.org

FAMM is an educational organization that works to repeal mandatory minimum sentences. It provides legislators, the public, and the media with information on and analyses of minimum-sentencing laws. FAMM publishes the quarterly newsletter *FAMM-gram*.

The Heritage Foundation
214 Massachusetts Ave. NE, Washington, DC 20002-4999
(202) 546-4400 • (800) 544-4843 • fax: (202) 544-6979
e-mail: pubs@heritage.org • website: http://www.heritage.org

The Heritage Foundation is a conservative public policy research institute. It is a proponent of limited government and advocates tougher sentencing and the construction of more prisons. The foundation publishes articles on a variety of public policy issues in its Backgrounder series and in its quarterly journal *Policy Review*.

The John Howard Society of Canada
771 Montreal St., Kingston, ON K7K 3J6 CANADA
(613) 542-7547 • fax: (613) 542-6824
e-mail: national@johnhoward.ca • website: http://www.johnhoward.ca

The John Howard Society of Canada advocates reform of the criminal justice system and monitors governmental policy to ensure fair and compassionate treatment of prisoners. It views imprisonment as a last-resort option. The organization provides education to the community, support services to at-risk youth, and rehabilitation programs to former inmates. Its publications include the booklet *Literacy and the Courts: Protecting the Right to Understand*.

National Center on Institutions and Alternatives (NCIA)
3125 Mt. Vernon Ave., Alexandria, VA 22305
(703) 684-0373 • fax: (703) 684-6037
e-mail: ncia@igc.apc.org • website: http://www.ncianet.org/ncia

NCIA works to reduce the number of people institutionalized in prisons and mental hospitals. It favors the least restrictive forms of detention for juvenile murderers, and it opposes sentencing juveniles as adults and executing juvenile murderers. NCIA publishes the book *Juve-*

nile Decarceration: The Politics of Correctional Reform, and the booklet Scared Straight: Second Look.

National Crime Prevention Council (NCPC)
1700 K St. NW, 2nd Fl., Washington, DC 20006-3817
(202) 261-4111 • fax: (202) 296-1356
e-mail: webmaster@ncpc.org • website: http://www.ncpc.org

The NCPC provides training and technical assistance to groups and individuals interested in crime prevention. It advocates job training and recreation programs as means to reduce youth crime and violence. The council, which sponsors the Take a Bite Out of Crime campaign, publishes the book Preventing Violence: Program Ideas and Examples, the booklet How Communities Can Bring Up Youth Free from Fear and Violence, and the newsletter Catalyst, which is published ten times a year.

National Institute of Justice (NIJ)
National Criminal Justice Reference Service (NCJRS)
Box 6000, Rockville, MD 20849
(301) 519-5500 • (800) 851-3420
e-mail: askncjrs@ncjrs.org • website: http://www.ncjrs.org

A component of the Office of Justice Programs of the U.S. Department of Justice, the NIJ supports research on crime, criminal behavior, and crime prevention. The National Criminal Justice Reference Service acts as a clearinghouse that provides information and research about criminal justice. Its publications include the research briefs Crime in the Schools: A Problem-Solving Approach, and Violence Among Middle School and High School Students: Analysis and Implications for Prevention.

National Rifle Association of America (NRA)
11250 Waples Mill Rd., Fairfax, VA 22030
(703) 267-1000 • fax: (703) 267-3989
website: http://www.nra.org

The NRA, with nearly 3 million members, is America's largest organization of gun owners. It is the primary lobbying group for those who oppose gun control laws. The NRA believes that such laws violate the U.S. Constitution and do nothing to reduce crime. In addition to its monthly magazines American Rifleman, American Hunter, and Incites, the NRA publishes numerous books, bibliographies, reports, and pamphlets on gun ownership, gun safety, and gun control.

Violence Policy Center (VPC)
2000 P St. NW, Suite 200, Washington, DC 20036
(202) 822-8200 • fax: (202) 822-8205
e-mail: comment@vpc.org • website: http://www.vpc.org

The center is an educational foundation that conducts research on firearms violence. It works to educate the public concerning the dangers of guns and supports gun-control measures. The center's publications include the report "Cease Fire: A Comprehensive Strategy to Reduce Firearms Violence" and the books NRA: Money, Firepower, and Fear and Assault Weapons and Accessories in America.

BIBLIOGRAPHY OF BOOKS

William J. Bennett, John J. DiIulio Jr., and John P. Walters — *Body Count: Moral Poverty . . . and How to Win America's War Against Crime and Drugs.* New York: Simon & Schuster, 1996.

William J. Bratton with Peter Knobler — *Turnaround: How America's Top Cop Reversed the Crime Epidemic.* New York: Random House, 1998.

Steven R. Donziger, ed. — *The Real War on Crime: The Report of the National Criminal Justice Commission.* New York: HarperPerennial, 1996.

Mansfield B. Frazier — *From Behind the Wall: Commentary on Crime, Punishment, and the Underclass by a Prison Inmate.* New York: Paragon House, 1995.

James Gilligan — *Violence: Our Deadly Epidemic and Its Causes.* New York: G.P. Putnam, 1996.

Dennis A. Henigan, E. Bruce Nicholson, and David Hemenway — *Guns and the Constitution: The Myth of Second Amendment Protection for Firearms in America.* Northampton, MA: Alethia Press, 1995.

Edward Humes — *No Matter How Loud I Shout: A Year in the Life of Juvenile Court.* New York: Simon & Schuster, 1996.

Wendy Kaminer — *It's All the Rage: Crime and Culture.* Reading, MA: Addison-Wesley, 1995.

Don B. Kates and Gary Kleck — *The Great American Gun Debate: Essays on Firearms and Violence.* San Francisco: Pacific Research Institute, 1997.

George L. Kelling and Catherine M. Coles — *Fixing Broken Windows: Restoring Order and Reducing Crime in Our Communities.* New York: Martin Kessler Books, 1996.

Randall Kennedy — *Race, Crime, and the Law.* New York: Pantheon, 1997.

David J. Krajicek — *Scooped! Media Miss Real Story on Crime While Chasing Sex, Sleaze, and Celebrities.* New York: Columbia University Press, 1998.

John R. Lott Jr. — *More Guns, Less Crime: Understanding Crime and Gun-Control Laws.* Chicago: University of Chicago Press, 1998.

Edwin Meese III and Robert E. Moffit, eds. — *Making America Safer: What Citizens and Their State and Local Officials Can Do to Combat Crime.* Washington, DC: Heritage Foundation, 1997.

Steven F. Messner and Richard Rosenfeld — *Crime and the American Dream.* Belmont, CA: Wadsworth Publishing, 1997.

Katheryn K. Russell   *The Color of Crime: Racial Hoaxes, White Fear, Black Protectionism, Police Harassment, and Other Macroaggressions.* New York: New York University Press, 1998.

Michael Tonry   *Malign Neglect: Race, Crime, and Punishment in America.* New York: Oxford University Press, 1996.

Ved Varma, ed.   *Violence in Children and Adolescents.* Bristol, PA: Jessica Kingsley Publishers, 1997.

Willie L. Williams with Bruce B. Henderson   *Taking Back Our Streets: Fighting Crime in America.* New York: Scribner, 1996.

James Q. Wilson and Joan Petersilia, eds.   Crime. San Francisco: ICS Press, 1995.

Franklin Zimring and Gordon Hawkins   *Crime Is Not the Problem: Lethal Violence in America.* New York: Oxford University Press, 1997.

INDEX

5 - 3/53